Red Letter Day · My Redheaded Friend ·

Cherry in Sherry · The Red

Red Road · The Red Sea's

In · Are You Seeing Red? · Bloody Mary · The

Chick Is a Communist (1940s jive-talk) · White

Cylinder Week · Mother Nature's Gift · Woman's

Friend · It's Raining Down South · I Fell Off the

Roof · I've Got My Flowers · I've Got My

Friend · I've Got the Grannies · Lady in the Red

Dress · Grandma's Here · Somebody's Visiting ·

Tante Rosa Kommt aus Amerika (aunt rosa is

coming from america—german) · My Redheaded Aunt

from Red Bank · Aunt Red from Potsdam's Here

· Communists in the Summer House (norwegian) ·

Aunt Susie · Aunt Flo Is Visiting · Aunt Tilly

Is Here

The Curse

The Curse

CONFRONTING

THE LAST

UNMENTIONABLE

TABOO:

MENSTRUATION

KAREN HOUPPERT

Farrar, Straus and Giroux

NEW YORK

Farrar, Straus and Giroux
19 Union Square West, New York 10003

Copyright © 1999 by Karen Houppert
All rights reserved
Distributed in Canada by Douglas & McIntyre Ltd.
Printed in the United States of America
Designed by Abby Kagan
First edition, 1999

Library of Congress Cataloging-in-Publication Data
Houppert, Karen, 1956–
    The curse : confronting the last unmentionable taboo: menstruation
    / Karen Houppert. — 1st ed.
        p.   cm.
    ISBN 0-374-27366-9 (alk. paper)
    1. Menstruation—Social aspects.   2. Menstruation—Public opinion.
    I. Title.
    GN484.38.H68   1999
    612.6'62—dc21   98-45364

See pages 257–258 for Permissions

FOR KIA

Contents

CONTENTS

PART THREE

The Adult: P.M.S. the Scourge of the Nineties 139

PART FOUR

Unlikely Prophets: The Menstrual Counterculture 197

The Curse

WELCOME THIS NEW DAY FOR WOMANHOOD

This summer you can experience a comfort and an assurance of daintiness you have never known before

Tampax eliminates the discomfort and irritation of external sanitary napkins. You are socially unconscious of it always.

SANITARY PROTECTION WORN INTERNALLY

Tampax eliminates chafing, odor and embarrassment, insures protection is complete and internal. Tampax permits daintiness at all times.

IT SEEMS too good, too impossible to be true. But ...at last...a method of sanitary protection has been perfected that enables you to be completely free of embarrassment...completely comfortable... completely sure of safe protection.

Tampax eliminates the external sanitary pad entirely. It is known to the medical profession as a tampon. Small, compressed, highly absorbent, made of surgical cotton, *Tampax is worn internally.*

Your doctor will be the first to tell you that Tampax is the most natural and the most hygienic method of sanitary protection ... accepted for advertising by the American Medical Association.

Thousands of women have already tried Tampax and would no sooner go back to the old-fashioned napkin than they would to the methods in use fifteen years ago.

Tampax is quite simple to use and it provides a freedom and daintiness never before possible. No belts. No pins. No pads. No chafing. No binding. Tampax eliminates odor *because it prevents its formation.* Tampax provides complete sanitary protection...safe at all times. It stays in place, through the utmost strenuous sports, yet it can be removed in a moment's time. *And you are totally unconscious of it.*

A month's supply of Tampax comes in a purse-size package. You can buy it at drug and department stores everywhere. Complete instructions for use are included. *PACKAGE OF TEN* 35¢

Tampax is sure. It stays in place though you exercise strenuously, yet it can be removed in a moment's time.

Exclusive Advantages of Tampax

Each Tampax is enclosed in a convenient and patented applicator, sealed in an individual wrapper. The fingers never touch the cotton. Easier to use, daintiness is always assured, and there is no doubt about effective protection and comfort.

Tampax cannot disintegrate. It is made of specially compressed, highly absorbent, long-fibred surgical cotton. Though very small when inserted, on contact with moisture it gently expands to that, although you are completely unconscious of it, one Tampax will absorb one to two ounces, the equivalent of a third of a glass of water.

FOR PHYSICIANS—the facts probably read about Tampax in the medical journals or are completely familiar with it through your hospital or some other source. If however, you would like to know more about Tampax, we will gladly send you literature and information as described in the Journal of the American Medical Association. Address: Tampax Incorporated, New Brunswick, N. J.

Tampax is completely invisible, for it is worn internally.

ACCEPTED FOR ADVERTISING BY THE AMERICAN MEDICAL ASSOCIATION

Introduction

began researching menstruation in 1995 because I was miffed. Not because I was worried about the possible health risks associated with tampon use (maybe I'd heard about some olden-days disease called toxic shock syndrome, but never of a *dioxin* connection), or because I thought a compelling feminist analysis lurked beneath the surface (what have periods got to do with politics?), or because I hoped to challenge menstrual taboos (of course we don't talk about bleeding in polite society; why should we?). The ignoble sentiment motivating my investigation was parsimony. I was an irritated consumer. Tambrands, makers of Tampax, had just reduced the number of plugs in a box from forty to thirty-two *and* raised the price. The snips!

"What's the deal?" I wondered. And as I posed that question, I tumbled headlong into the netherworld of feminine hygiene ads, menstrual etiquette, period-product focus groups, bodily effluents and environmental effluents, hormones, scents, sex, and surfactants. I surfaced with the preliminary results of my foray in a 1995 *Village Voice* article titled "Embarrassed to Death: The Hidden Dangers of the Tampon Industry"[1] and then dove back in. Some three years later, I emerged with this profound analogy: Blood is kinda like snot. How come it's not treated that way?

People with runny noses do not hide their tissues from colleagues and family members. They do not die of embarrassment when they sneeze in public. Young girls do not cringe if a boy spies them buying a box of Kleenex. Caught without a hanky on a cold day, people sometimes use their sleeves; they are sheepish but not humiliated. They do not blush or stammer or hide the evidence. No one celebrates congestion. It is inconvenient and occasionally, when accompanied by a cold, decidedly unpleasant. But those who suffer publicly—*ah-choo!*—are casually blessed. It is, in essence, no big deal.

The same is not true of periods.

And yet the facts seem equally straightforward: Once a month, the lining of the uterus, acting on signals from estrogen and progesterone hormones, thickens with spongy, blood-filled nutrients. If the woman has had sex and an egg and a sperm join, this uterine lining (endometrium) will be used to sustain the developing embryo. If fertilization doesn't take place, the egg travels down the fallopian tube, through the uterus, past the cervix, and out the vagina. Approximately twelve days later, when the levels of estrogen and progesterone have dropped and the uterus has gotten the message that no pregnancy has occurred, the uterine lining—blood and mucus—simply flows out. In total, each period consists of four to six tablespoons of blood.

Such simple biological facts seem inconsistent with the elaborate machinations we go through to hide the fact that we're bleeding. Yet for most women, the menstrual etiquette we follow is so ingrained that we never question it. Of course, we would never mention to our father-in-law that the reason we really, really, really need him to pull the car over at a rest area is because we need to change a tampon. "What would be the point of offending him?" we think, instead of "Why would this be considered offensive?" Menstrual etiquette is so habitual with us, we barely even think about it.

In fact, *nobody* spends time thinking about periods. Research on Americans' attitudes toward menstruation is very hard to come by. Periods are not a popular dissertation topic. Prestige and altruism rarely drive scientists to seek new cures for cramps. The U.S. government, which has only recently recognized the importance of studying women's health issues by creating the National Institutes of Health's Office of Women's Health, mostly limits its analysis of menstruation to one question: Does it render women unfit for combat? (The United States Army's Human Engineering Laboratory published a bibliography in 1980 titled *Human Performance: Women in Nontraditional Occupations and the Influence of the Menstrual Cycle*; it cited 1,485 studies.[2]) The Society for Menstrual Cycle Research, a collective of academics who recognized the importance of such work as long ago as 1979, has the most comprehensive collection of data. But Society members are the first to lament the dearth of research attention—and dollars—devoted to this topic. When the experts do focus their attention on menstruation, it's to emphasize its pathology: premenstrual syndrome. While studies on healthy women are hard to come by, studies on angry, depressed, and unreasonable women fill the pages of professional journals.

Meanwhile, it is safe to assume that some large-scale national studies about American attitudes toward menstruation are being conducted by the menstrual products industry. But they're not sharing. "These studies are of a competitive nature," explains Elaine Plummer, a spokesperson for Procter & Gamble. The company with the largest share of the tampon and sanitary pad markets, P&G solicits this kind of information as part of its standard marketing research. "But that information isn't something we'd want to make public," Plummer says.

In all of menstrual history, the solitary exception to this industry-wide policy is a major national survey conducted by Tampax in 1981. For some reason, Tampax uncharacteristically shared copies of the report with interested parties—who, incidentally, were not all that many people. The Society for Menstrual Cycle Research has a copy; I found another languishing in the stacks of the library of the Sex Information and Education Council of the United States in New York City. The report is eighteen years old, but it gives us a starting point.

In April and May of 1981, fifty trained researchers conducted 15-minute phone interviews with more than a thousand men and women across the country. The study, designed by a company called Research & Forecasts, Inc., included people of all ages, education levels, income levels, and ethnicities. The results of the survey were startling. Pollsters discovered that men and women had similar beliefs about menstruation, sharing an overall attitude that the researchers characterized as "negative" and an understanding of menstruation that was "confused." More than one-quarter thought that women could not function normally at work while menstruating, with 8 percent (that would have been 14 million Americans!) saying that women should make an effort to stay away from others when they're having their periods. Thirty-five percent said they thought menstruation affected a woman's ability to think, 30 percent thought women should cut down on their physical activities while menstruating, 49 percent said that women had a different scent at that time, and 27 percent said menstruating women looked different. Half thought women shouldn't have sexual intercourse during their periods, and 22 percent believed swimming while menstruating was harmful. Two-thirds of those surveyed said that women should not mention their periods in the office or in social situations—that included veiled references to cramps or headaches—and more than one-third thought women should conceal the fact that they're menstruating from their families (for example, by hiding sanitary products). Interestingly, men were more likely than women to think it was okay to talk openly about periods (38 percent, as opposed to 27 percent). Thirty-one percent of the women surveyed reported not knowing what menstruation was the first time they got their periods, and 43 percent of the women had had negative responses to their first period, saying that they felt scared, confused, terrible, panicky, or ill.

Today, many women begin a conversation about menstruation with a sigh of relief. "Thank God we're more open about these things than my mother's generation," they tell me when they learn I am writing a book about the topic. There is a sense that attitudes are changing rapidly; that feminism has allowed women to think about their bodies differently and that taboos about menstruation have benefited from this détente. They *have* benefited, but the attitudes reflected in the Tampax report are not so quaint and antiquated as we might think. Using other cultural barometers—ads, teen magazines, newspaper

articles, popular literature, and recent, narrowly focused studies—I discovered that these myths persist. Things have
changed somewhat, but there have been no radical leaps in
our menstrual consciousness in the past two decades. And
in the peculiarly mapped landscape of menstrual etiquette,
where beliefs are based on superstition, shame, and sexual self-
consciousness, it seems unlikely that the intervening years of
inattention have fomented a sea change in attitudes.

But who cares? What difference does it make if women want to
keep their bleeding private? Or if men want to keep women's
bleeding private? Or if the social contract includes a menstrual
etiquette rider whereby all parties agree that bleeding is a nasty
business best kept quiet?

In a *Glamour* magazine item about my 1995 *Village Voice*
piece, a reporter questioned whether women really needed to
push the outside of *that* envelope. In particular, the journalist
focused on the cover of the issue of *The Village Voice* that
featured my article (as did most of those writing letters to the paper, who found our cover photo offensive). In fact, the picture
looked like any of a dozen provocative ads for skin creams, perfumes, or health clubs: a woman's sexy lower torso in profile,
smooth thighs and pert butt alluringly displayed. But here, peek-
ing out from between the woman's thighs, was a tampon string.

People freaked. And, like the *Glamour* reporter—and a *New
York Times* reporter who wondered whether anything was still
sacred after that image—they couldn't get past the cover to the
article inside. Which was, and is, my point. These taboos matter because they prevent consumer debate and scientific re-

search, as well as safety monitoring of the sanitary protection industry. And, by defining how women think and talk about menstruation, men—the mostly male CEOs of companies manufacturing menstrual products, as well as advertising executives, religious leaders, and sex-ed authors—have set a tone that shapes women's experiences for them, defining what they are allowed to feel about their periods, what they are allowed to feel about their bodies, and what they are allowed to feel about their sexuality. Menstrual etiquette matters because women are being manipulated. The consequences are significant.

If the sole conversation a girl has with her mother about "down there" consists of a quick, covert discussion of sanitary protection logistics, if her teachers are secretive and vague as they line her and her fifth-grade girlfriends up for the sole public acknowledgement of periods, "The Movie," and if every ad she ever sees reminds her that the worst possible thing would be for boys to discover that she bleeds, she is sure to think there is something wrong with the event (a curse?) or herself.

What does it mean for a girl, or woman, to say simply, "This happens to me" and for society to say, "No it doesn't." Not in movies. Not in books. Not in conversations.

After a while, it becomes psychologically disorienting to look out at a world where your reality does not exist. I am not suggesting that society's attitude toward menstruation creates this phenomenon all by itself. But menstrual etiquette is an element of a woman's experience that contributes to this disorienting effect. It complements a barrage of distorted images and stories about women's bodies that we face daily. Because ideas about menstruation tie into prevailing notions that women's bodies are dangerously permeable, they become part of the controlling myths our culture has spun to manipulate our perceptions of ourselves and our sexuality.

In the following four essays, I examine how our culture conspires to transform monthly bleeding from a benign inconvenience into a shameful, embarrassing, and even debilitating event.

PART ONE

The Industry

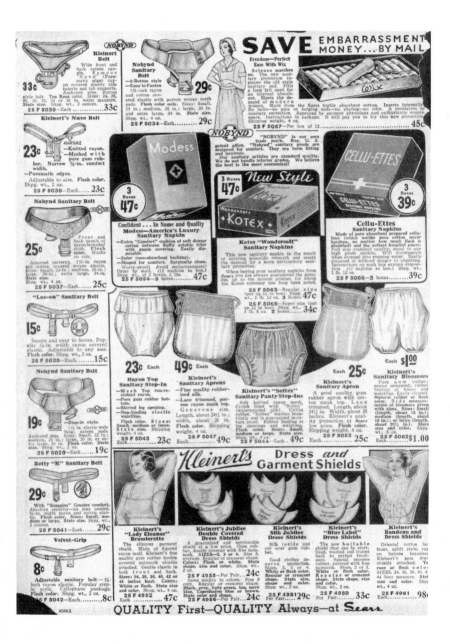

Our only interest is in protecting you.
—*Tampax ad, 1972*

"Welcome this new day for womanhood," Tampax Inc. announces on July 26, 1936, in its very first mass-market ad. Describing a brave new world, the company boasts that "thousands of women have already tried Tampax and would no sooner go back to the old-fashioned napkin than they would to the methods in use fifteen years ago." Asserting a year later that this is "a comfort never known before," the company crows over a "woman's world—remade" and says, "After 2000 years . . . of the woman alone with her troublesome days . . . suddenly it happened!"

Sixty years later, Tambrands Inc.—same company, different name—was the leading manufacturer of tampons, cornering 55 percent of an astonishing $8 billion market worldwide. Clearly, July 1936 was a liberating moment for women. The promise of "No belts. No pins. No pads. No chafing. No binding" was irresistible. Like today's tampon ads, the earliest ones celebrated active women, shown riding horses, dancing, playing tennis, and sunbathing. Freedom and comfort were hyped. And women bought. Still, Tampax wasn't content with marketing convenience. Like others in the sanitary protection industry, it took care to remind women that menstruation was naughty; as irrepressible evidence of sexuality, news of its arrival, departure, and duration had to be kept under wraps.

A journey through the coded history of sanitary protection makes for a fascinating crash course in American sexuality—and its repression. Shame and secrecy are the primary message. One 1930s Kotex tampon was even named Fibs, and every sanitary protection ad reinforces the notion that the ultimate humiliation would be any indication that you're menstruating. Full of dire warnings about "accidents" and assurances of the invisibility of their products, sanitary protection ads typically promise, as this 1949 *Good Housekeeping* example did, "You don't know you're wearing one—and neither does anyone else."

Forget the natural dismay of discovering you've bled through your skivvies to your skirt: these ads zeroed in on women's fear of exposure, promoting a whole culture of concealment. Tapping into that taboo, ads reinforced the idea that any sign that you were menstruating, even purchasing menstrual products, was cause for embarrassment. "Women of refinement dislike to ask for so intimate an article by its full descriptive name," Kotex reminded store owners in a 1921 trade publication. Applauding its ingenuity, the company bragged, "Kotex advertising to women is so restrained in tone that women's intuition tells them what Kotex is! Not once, in any advertisement to women, have we described Kotex as a sanitary napkin." Tampax always offered to send a trial package "in a plain wrapper." And today Kimberly-Clark advertises an applicator-free tampon "wrapped in outrageous colors" by depicting a model who wears the tampons as curlers, while the copy reminds readers how embarrassing it is to reach into a handbag for lipstick and pull out a tampon, and the headline pledges, "Only you'll know what they're really for."

Advertisers have long tipped women off to the nature of their products by using code words. For example, a 1934 Sears catalog ad illustrates eighteen different kinds of "sanitary" products, yet never once says what they're for. The headline simply announces, "Save embarrassment, money . . . by mail." The spread offers eight different belts, poetically named to sound like racehorses—Velvet-Grip, Betty "K," Lox-on—and rivaling Anne Rice's imagination for their creative S&M configurations of straps, clips, and belts. Also for sale: "pure gum rubber bloomers," "worry-proof" pads, and rubber "sanitary aprons" (worn under skirts but over derrières, and weighted with lead to keep from bunching). There is "liquid-proof underwear" and, because "science marches on," a brand-new tampon called Wix.

These products were hyped as the hottest new scientific inventions. Referring to an American love affair with science that really gained momentum at the turn of the century, Barbara Ehrenreich and Deirdre English, authors of *For Her Own Good*, describe the ascendancy of germ theory and a culture of cleanliness that seeped into the popular psyche: "For the Domestic Science experts, the Germ Theory of Disease pointed the way to their first victory: the transformation of cleaning from a matter of dilettantish dusting to a sanitary crusade against 'dangerous enemies within.'"[1] Clearly, the companies peddling new menstrual products hoped to capitalize on that trend. "I like the scientific background of Tampax (it was invented by a doctor)," one 1940s testimonial in *Good Housekeeping* read. And, in 1946, Modess even put out a product called Meds—

"Go Meds . . . Go Merrier!"—and told reticent customers to "ask any nurse!" Always describing their products as "sanitary," asserting that they were made of "surgical cotton" and "hygienically sealed in individual containers," manufacturers played to germ paranoia, boasting that millions of "modern women" were converts. (In fact, the chemicals used in sterilization proved harmful and the process was discontinued.)

In the 1930s, though, medical expertise was pitted against religious expertise. Priests in the Catholic Church objected to the use of tampons. They worried that women would find them erotic. And they worried that girls would lose their virginity upon insertion. (Their other concern: all those women and girls using their fingers to go exploring "down there." Who knows what they might learn along the way?) Priests denounced Tampax in print. But Tampax summoned the forces of medical science and modern technology to stand against such outdated traditionalism. Not only was the tampon invented by a doctor, the ads made perfectly clear, but the packaging prominently displayed a red cross and bore the slogan "Accepted for Advertising by the American Medical Association." Of course, the product wasn't approved or endorsed by the AMA; it only appeared in the *Journal of the American Medical Association* as a paid advertisement. But Tampax's founder and president, Ellery Mann, believed the tag line lent "an ethical as well as a medical background to the product." (In 1943, at the Federal Trade Commission's request, Tampax dropped the phrase.[2]) As time passed, Tampax continued to capitalize on popular movements and today plugs its products as environmentally friendly. "Think green," it urges in a 1991 ad, reminding women that the applicator is biodegradable.

Sanitary protection companies also vied for popular personalities to sell their products. In the 1980s such notables as Cathy Rigby frolicked in telling white leotards, and in the 1960s a teenage pre-Partridge Susan Dey strolled merrily across an airport tarmac touting the virtues of Tampax. There is even a classic 1928 *McCall's* ad featuring an Edward Steichen photograph of Lee Miller, who would later become Man Ray's lover, a World War II photographer, and a *Life* staffer. Newly arrived in the city, a young Miller met up with Steichen and modeled for stock photos that were bought by Kotex. Unbeknownst to Miller, she would become the first live model ever to appear in a "sanitary protection" ad. According to biographers, she wasn't flattered by the distinction.

But even in the 1990s, celebrities are loath to be known as, for example, the Stayfree Girl. In 1997, Johnson & Johnson tried to line up a spokesperson for its launch of a new pad with "walls" (similar to P&G's Always with channels). According to a McCann-Erickson ad agency insider who didn't want her name used, they had a tough time finding a model. "They went to athletes, film stars, TV stars, and the majority of people refused," she explained. "They didn't want to be associated with a maxipad." J&J approached Olympic figure skater Nancy Kerrigan, who agreed to let them use her likeness—footage of her skating, etc.—but refused to discuss the product herself in any advertising. They then went after the Spice Girls, thinking that their "Tell me what you want, what you really, really want" lyrics had the kind of hip sensibility to attract younger women. "But even this group, all about girl power, wanted nothing to do with pads," the McCann staffer said. In fact, J&J, makers of baby powder and No More Tears shampoo, didn't even want its own name, as the parent company, attached to the product. "When we were talking in a meeting about using a celebrity to leverage the product, someone asked why we don't use the J&J name," the staffer recalled. "And the company representatives said, 'Absolutely not!'"

Is there something about bleeding that would soil J&J's pristine baby-powder image? Johnson & Johnson spokesperson John McKeegan said this refusal to identify J&J with a menstrual product was standard for the company. "It's not quite as simple as saying this would tarnish J&J's name," he explained. "This is just a long-standing decision regarding the J&J name and what it's associated with. More than anything else, J&J is known through its baby products and through its medical products. And the decision was, that's where the name would remain." (Citing company policy, he refused to comment on Stayfree's frustrating search for a celebrity spokesperson.)

Clearly no one wants to be associated with bleeding. Even in its first ad, Tampax stokes this anxiety. "Tampax eliminates chafing, odor, and embarrassment . . . permits daintiness at all times." And this theme of confidentiality—your menstruation is our little secret—remains a Tampax staple, right up to its 1990s "Trust Is Tampax" campaign, which promises, "No one will ever know you've got your period."

Such secrecy has its advantages.

THE TAMPON-DIOXIN LINK: SHOULD WE WORRY?

In 1992, a congressional subcommittee charged with overseeing the Food and Drug Administration stumbled on an exchange of memos regarding reports the FDA had declined to make public. It seems several FDA scientists had discovered trace levels of dioxin, a potentially harmful by-product of the chlorine-bleaching process at paper and wood-pulp mills, in some commercially produced tampons. (Most tampons today contain rayon, a wood-pulp derivative.) Citing studies that indicated dioxin was unsafe at any level—not only potentially carcinogenic, but toxic to the immune system and a cause of birth defects—subcommittee chair Ted Weiss, a Democrat from New York, accused the FDA of purposely downplaying the dangers to women by ignoring one of its own scientist's warnings. Weiss's staff had uncovered a March 1989 FDA memo stating that the risk of dioxin in tampons "can be quite high." While the memo advised that "the most effective risk-management strategy would be to assure that tampons . . . contain no dioxin," the FDA never tested tampons. Furthermore, the agency felt confident deleting the following sentence from its final report on dioxin and medical devices: "It appears that the most significant risks may occur in tampon products."[3]

At the time, *The Wall Street Journal* was one of the few papers to cover the hearing—though its 10-inch article (June 11, 1992) was given little play, running on page B-8. After all, dioxin's toxicity was still being hotly disputed by scientists. And tampons were hardly a priority. For the most part, dioxin was—and is today—studied in terms of the effluent that pulp and paper plants release into the waterways. Through fish and birds who have ingested dioxin in water, the chemical travels up the food chain by way of fat cells, where it's stored. It has been discovered, for example, in particularly high quantities in the breast milk of women who eat a lot of fish. Despite growing

evidence of dioxin's toxic potential, all pulp and paper manufacturers, many scientists, and most FDA officials argued for
years that there were "acceptable levels" of dioxin. Though it
had proven to be a carcinogen in animals, they insisted that its
exact low-level effect on humans remained unknown.

Called on the carpet by Weiss's committee, Melvin Stratmeyer, chief of the health sciences branch of the FDA,
defended the agency's silence on the tampon-dioxin connection. Tampons pose absolutely no health risk for women, he insisted. How did he know? The FDA had researched the issue
and analyzed the link between dioxin and tampons. But if they
did not actually test any tampons for dioxin—as Stratmeyer
freely admitted—where did the raw data supporting this conclusion come from? It was supplied by the tampon industry.

And what did the tampon industry have to say? When
confronted specifically about the dioxin present in tampons,
a Tambrands spokesperson, Bruce Garren, assured *The Wall
Street Journal* in 1992 that "there [are] no significant dioxin
levels in our product."[4] The tampon-dioxin connection,
pointed out in a few FDA memos, played out as a blip on the
screen—underreported and largely forgotten in subsequent in-
vestigations of dioxin.

But in September 1995, the Environmental Protection
Agency began preparing a new report on dioxin that suggested
the threshold level for dioxin damage was considerably lower
than previously believed. In fact, the document, formally released to the public in 1997, suggests there are no "acceptable
levels" of dioxin. Drawing on the results of scientific research
around the world—from sources as diverse as a U.S. Air Force

study that documented decreased testis size in men exposed to dioxin and a University of South Florida study that saw a connection between dioxin exposure and endometriosis in monkeys—it's clear that tests are showing something even more important than the potential carcinogenic link: dioxin, in levels once thought acceptably low, affects the reproductive and immune systems. There is evidence that dioxin may be linked to lower sperm counts in men, a higher probability of endometriosis in women, and a depressed immune system in both.

Without suggesting any specific policy goals regarding dioxin emission, the authors of the EPA report frankly admit that pinpointing an acceptable exposure level is almost irrelevant. Given that dioxin is cumulative and slow to disintegrate, the real danger comes from repeated contact. And because dioxin is so prevalent—in the air, in the waterways, in the food chain, in paper products—effective regulation would have to be coordinated and pervasive. The EPA report, titled "A Health Assessment Document for Dioxin," forever changed the way people think about the chemical. In 1995, as word of the report spread, denials flew.

Asked again about the presence of dioxin in Tampax tampons, Garren said, "Chlorine is used in creating the rayon in tampons; however, no residue of that is left in tampons." He then conceded that tampons contain "trace levels" of dioxin but insisted that dioxin is a "natural product," as indicated by its presence in forest-fire residue. (Greenpeace counters that studies of ancient artifacts have shown that dioxin does not occur in nature, and dismisses the forest-fire example by describing how dioxin-laden pesticides, polluted water sources, and smog probably account for the dioxin in a forest.) Johnson & Johnson spokesperson John McKeegan went a little further by offering specific numbers for dioxin levels in his company's tampons. "The levels of dioxin in o.b.'s range from unde-tectable to 0.2 parts per trillion," he claims, asserting that this is well within EPA guidelines. (In fact, the 1995 EPA dioxin re-port declined to define "acceptable" dioxin levels.) And Tam-brands' Garren was similarly emphatic: "I believe dioxin in tampons poses absolutely no public health threat."

With no reliable government regulation, this may be the only reassurance women get. And while it's true that the level of dioxin "normal Americans" encounter and consume on a daily basis makes tampons only one part of a larger, potentially more dangerous equation, women are hit with a double whammy. Seventy-three million menstruating women are bol-stering an industry that releases toxins into our air and water-ways. And seventy-three million American women may be directly accumulating toxins in their bodies via tampons. Con-sider five tampons a day, five days a month, for 38 menstruat-ing years. That's 11,400 tampons in a lifetime. And all of the major brands and sizes—Playtex, o.b., Tampax, Kotex—con-tain rayon.

Today, we may be seeing the most obvious effects of di-oxin exposure with infertility. According to the EPA, hormonal changes have been observed in humans who have only a little more dioxin in their bodies than the general population has.[5] The kinds of damage associated with dioxin exposure among males include reduced sperm count, testicular atrophy, abnor-mal testis structure, and smaller genitals. Among females, hormonal changes associated with dioxin have been linked to decreased fertility, an inability to maintain pregnancy, and ovarian dysfunction.

Also, several recent animal studies have suggested that the explosion in endometriosis among humans—more than five million American women suffer from this once-rare disease[6]—may be attributable to dioxin. While improved detection methods may account for some of the increase, dioxin's estrogen-mimicking traits are making it a likely suspect.

Endometriosis is a chronic disease that occurs when cells from the uterine lining migrate outside the uterus, mutating into growths or tumors in other parts of the pelvis—and even occasionally in other parts of the body. As the cells respond to menstrual hormones, they wax and wane with the body's rising and falling estrogen levels. The disease can be excruciatingly painful and cause internal bleeding, permanent scar tissue, and infertility. Recently, scientists conducting research on the long-term effects of dioxin on a colony of monkeys discovered that 79 percent of the female animals who had been exposed to dioxin developed endometriosis. The connection was widely reported, with articles appearing in *Science* and *Scientific American* as well as in scholarly journals.[7] And while most of the tests linking dioxin and endometriosis have been conducted on animals, scientists fear they are seeing the same effects in humans. For example, in a study of infertile patients at the Bikur Cholim Hospital in Jerusalem, 18 percent of the women with endometriosis tested dioxin-positive, as compared with only 3 percent in the control group (women with tubal infertility).[8]

Especially frightening are the minuscule amounts of dioxin

that are wreaking this hormonal havoc. For example, the monkeys with endometriosis were exposed to between 5 and 25 parts per trillion of dioxin, the equivalent of spitting in an Olympic-size pool.[9] Indeed, the potency of this toxin is such that the mere 30 pounds estimated to be released in the United States annually is enough to send scientists and environmentalists banging on the EPA's door begging for a "zero dioxin" policy.

The most disturbing evidence scientists present comes from a decades-long case study of the Great Lakes. In the 1950s, industrial waste high in organochlorines (dioxin is one member of the organochlorine family, which includes the contaminant Agent Orange and chemicals that were found at Love Canal) began to pile up in the Great Lakes, which, unlike most bodies of water, drains only about 1 percent of its volume annually. Over the years, scientists have linked these dioxin-like compounds to large-scale hormonal, reproductive, and developmental impairment in birds, fish, and wildlife. A few incidents, like a 1978 rice-oil contamination incident in Taiwan and a 1976 industrial accident in Seveso, Italy, have allowed them to trace the effects of heavy doses among humans. The damage they are seeing may be insignificant among adults but tends to surface in the offspring of the exposed population.[10] According to the EPA, dioxin crosses from the mother to the fetus across the placenta. Once born, babies continue to get an infusion of dioxin via breast milk. Because breast milk is highly contaminated, nursing babies consume between 4 and 12 percent of their entire lifetime dose in this crucial developmental year.[11]

Some scientists are even beginning to speculate that dioxin is contributing to the plummeting sperm counts recently documented in the U.S. and Europe. A 1997 National Academy of Sciences study—analyzing 61 published papers and endorsed by the National Institutes of Health—reported that sperm densities in the U.S. have been decreasing by 1.5 million sperm per milliliter (or 1.5 percent) per year since 1938. (In Europe, it's twice that rate, at 3.1 percent per year.) While the decline is slow and men obviously have plenty of sperm left, experts do worry about this as a barometer of general health. (Also, decreased sperm count can be a red flag for testicular cancer.) Shanna Swan, chief of reproductive epidemiology at the California Department of Health Services, who headed up the NAS study, suspects that persistent organic pollutants like dioxin are to blame.[12]

Because some of these changes occur with only a slight increase in the dioxin levels in a person's body, dioxin in any amount is worrisome. (And one study, conducted by Linda Birnbaum of the Systemic Toxicology Branch at the National Institute of Environmental Health Sciences, showed that low long-term doses of dioxin are actually more effectively absorbed through the skin than high doses.) The 1995 EPA report suggests that if there is any margin of safety between the average American's current dioxin level and the level where it begins to affect health, it is a small one. For example, the average American's dioxin level is estimated at 9 ng/kg (9 nanograms for every kilogram of body weight), and lower testosterone levels have been detected in people with dioxin levels of only 14 ng/kg. Greenpeace's Joe Thornton puts it this way: "Even if there is a safe dioxin dose, we are already at, near, or above that threshold. Additional exposures cannot be considered 'safe.'"[13]

As for the sanitary protection industry's insistence that the "trace levels" of dioxin found in their products pose absolutely no health threat, the truth is, they don't know. And neither does the FDA. The FDA bases its assurances on a 1990 report studying the link between dioxin and cancer. Tampons were one of the many wood-pulp and paper products studied, and the FDA relied on data provided by the tampon companies—without ever testing individual tampons or determining how "dermal contact" in the vagina might differ from regular dermal contact—to arrive at the conclusion that there was no cancer risk. "The estimated risks of cancer posed by dioxin over a lifetime's use were below 1 in 10 billion—far lower than the usual threshold for regulatory action," FDA deputy commissioner Carol Scheman wrote in a letter to the editor published in *The Wall Street Journal*.[14] Five years later, the EPA released its dioxin reassessment study, in which the authors concluded that they had been unable to identify an "acceptable" or "no-effect" dose of dioxin.

Worried that the federal agencies have glossed over the significance of dioxin in menstrual products—given the slew of other potential dioxin sources—Representative Carolyn Maloney, a Democrat from New York, introduced a bill on November 7, 1997, that would earmark money for the National Institutes of Health to thoroughly investigate the issue. (All of three reporters showed up for the press conference announcing the initiative.) Maloney is also demanding that all the ingredients in tampons—cottons sprayed with pesticides, perfumes, and other additives—be exhaustively tested for safety and that the results be made available to the public. "The shocking irony is that there has been far more testing on the possible health effects of chlorine-bleached coffee filters than on chlorine-bleached tampons," Maloney said, insisting that an independent agency, *not* the tampon industry, needed to conduct the tests.

Meanwhile, the sanitary protection industry and its pulp and paper suppliers defend themselves by myopically asserting that women need not worry about tampons that contain "trace levels" of the chemical, for example — instead of admitting that this is an absurd way to view the problem. What matters is how much dioxin women — and men — are exposed to over time. But the pulp-and-paper industry insists that the Environmental Protection Agency is simply wrong. "We don't believe there's any evidence that dioxin is a health hazard to humans," said Barry Polsky, spokesperson for the American Forest and Paper Association.

Long involved in the struggle to regulate dioxin emission, environmentalists have been through all this before. "Industry's tactic is simply to delay this thing as long as possible," says Greenpeace's Lisa Finaldi, explaining that the broad participation of internationally renowned scientists legitimizes the EPA study. "Obviously, pulp and paper manufacturers want to avoid the kinds of expensive changes a 'zero dioxin' policy would compel."

And the EPA is hardly cracking the whip. First the agency dragged its heels, taking years to compile and release its report. Then, when scientists presented irrefutable proof of dioxin's toxic effects, the EPA was finally forced to act. But instead of insisting that pulp and paper mills completely eliminate dioxin emissions, the agency issued regulations in 1998 that merely required manufacturers to cut back. While the hope is that this will reduce dioxin in the environment by 80 to 90 percent, the agency stopped short of requiring total elimination. The technology for a "zero dioxin" policy does exist, but it's costly—a $2.8 billion one-time conversion cost for the manufacturers, according to EPA estimates.[15] Worse yet, the agency is giving some pulp and paper manufacturers as long as fifteen years to get their act together for conversion.

According to environmental groups, a "90 percent dioxin-free" goal reflects an ideal world where there are adequate inspections, scrupulous corporations, and modern, state-of-the-art machinery that never breaks down. "Furthermore, the industry data looks only at two of the seventeen most toxic dioxin compounds," explains Rick Hinds, legislative director of the Greenpeace toxics campaign. "And many of these other dioxin compounds have been found in mills."

But the code of silence surrounding menstrual hygiene leaves consumers with little information and less clout. Consider the contemporary woman's relationship to the $1.7 billion sanitary protection industry. While we may have noticed that the number of tampons in a box dropped from forty to thirty-two in 1991—with no corresponding drop in price—protest mostly took the form of a moment's grousing in the feminine hygiene aisle. And as long as everything is so hush-hush, who chitchats about quality or safety? Who calls the industry or the FDA on the fact that consumers can read a list of ingredients on a shampoo bottle but not on a package of tampons, which are held for hours in one of the most porous and absorbent parts of a woman's body? Despite concern about dioxin, word hasn't exactly raced through the tampon-using community to spark consumer outrage. And while the federal government seems complicit (or at least complacent), who holds its officials accountable? Why are tampons not deemed a necessity but taxed, while everything from Trojans to cherry Chapstick is exempted? And finally, why are tampons five times the price (plus tax!) of the cotton balls they share supermarket shelves with? Who's getting rich off menstruation? And how far will they go to turn a profit?

A CASE STUDY: REVISITING TOXIC SHOCK

The tampon industry has a bad track record. In 1980, thirty-eight women died of tampon-related toxic shock syndrome, an event that might have been prevented were industry practices more carefully monitored.

Use of Procter & Gamble's Rely tampon was linked to these deaths, and its illustrious, if short-lived, career provides an instructive parallel to the dioxin threat. Procter & Gamble began distributing the tampon in test markets in 1975 and introduced the product to the general consumer in 1980 by mailing out sixty million free samples to women across the country. Made of superthirsty synthetics such as carboxymethylcellulose and polyester, Rely was billed as the most absorbent tampon ever to hit the market. As the product's popularity spread (it quickly stole 24 percent of the market), and as other tampon manufacturers introduced similar synthetics to stay competitive, the Centers for Disease Control began observing a strange phenomenon. Remarking on the 55 toxic shock–related deaths and the 1,066 cases of nonfatal TSS it had recorded since 1979, the agency observed in 1980 that this previously rare disease was surfacing primarily in young menstruating women.

How did the feminine hygiene industry respond to this news? With cover-ups and denials. Perhaps the most carefully chronicled investigation of the role corporations played in the toxic shock scandal appears in *Wall Street Journal* reporter Alecia Swasy's 1993 book *Soap Opera: The Inside Story of Procter & Gamble*. In it, Swasy details a management paper trail indicating that Procter & Gamble executives knew that there were problems with Rely years before they put it on the market. According to Swasy, a 1975 internal memo disclosed that components of the tampon were known cancer-causing agents and that the product also altered the populations of the natural microorganisms and bacteria found in the vagina. Though the company was receiving as many as 177 consumer complaints a month about Rely, it simply dismissed them, telling salespeople to do the same. "If asked, the salespeople were given canned answers that denied any link between tampons and toxic shock," Swasy reports. Though Procter & Gamble is often lauded for voluntarily withdrawing Rely from the market in September of 1980, it seems clear that the company didn't act until the FDA threatened to act for it. And the FDA didn't act until women died.[16]

After forcing Rely off the market—scientists had learned that the superthirsty synthetics provided an ideal breeding ground for the *Staphylococcus aureus* bacterium, which is present, though usually dormant, in the vaginas of 15 percent of all women—the FDA relaxed. For women and the tampon industry, the scare seemed to be over. As for the government, it left further research on the causes and effects of toxic shock syndrome to the tampon manufacturers, and the industry continued to escape any serious regulation.

The only exceptions to this neglect were two FDA requirements: the immediate requirement that tampon manufacturers advise consumers to choose tampons with the lowest possible effective absorbency and the long-delayed decision to require manufacturers to standardize their ranges of absorbency. Since toxic shock is tied to higher absorbencies, a national watchdog group called Public Citizen had urged the FDA for years to regulate absorbency labeling on tampon packages. These advocates argued that an FDA requirement that tampon manufacturers warn women — on the box — to use the lowest suitable absorbency had little relevance for consumers who had no way of actually knowing just how one product's absorbency related to another's. Lacking an industry standard — for example, o.b. "regulars" were actually more absorbent than Playtex "supers" — how could women tell whether they were buying a tampon with the lowest possible absorbency?

It took the FDA until 1990, after toxic shock had hit an estimated 60,000 women, to implement these new criteria. While tampon absorbencies are now standardized — for example, a "regular" tampon must fall within an absorbency range of 6 to 9 grams — Public Citizen had hoped for much more. It had also lobbied the FDA to require complete ingredient labeling on tampon packages. Not surprisingly, the FDA declined to require such labeling. An FDA spokesperson explained the agency's reasoning this way: "Medical devices [like tampons] contain a voluminous number of ingredients, in some cases enough to fill a small book, making it impractical to list ingredients on the box or label." (Unlike, say, the ingredients listed on a package of hot dogs or Twinkies.) The agency doesn't even require new-product testing for most tampons; unless they're substantially different from the standard, they are grandfathered. This allows same-shape/different-content products like Rely to be introduced under a speedier, less thorough approval process than brand-new medical devices. Some scientists even speculate that this relaxed approval process has allowed toxic shock–inducing products to remain on the market today.

According to Dr. Philip Tierno, Jr., director of microbiology and diagnostic immunology at Tisch Hospital/NYU Medical Center, and Dr. Bruce Hanna, associate professor of pathology at NYU Medical Center, who have conducted dozens of studies on tampons and published the results in journals like *Infectious Diseases in Obstetrics and Gynecology*, there may still be problems with the materials in tampons. They tested twenty varieties of tampons and concluded that, while all-cotton tampons produced none of the deadly TSS toxins, all other tampon products—including Playtex, o.b., Tampax, and Kotex brands—amplified the production of the toxins.

Wondering if the sudden surge in cases of toxic shock syndrome in 1980 corresponded with a shift in ingredients—by 1980 every single tampon on the market had one or more synthetic ingredients in it—Tierno had begun testing tampons in the early 1980s. He realized there could be only three possible explanations for the increase in TSS: either women had changed, or the toxins had changed, or the tampon had changed. Looking at earlier CDC and state health department tests documenting varieties of antibodies found in women's blood, he confirmed that women's bodies had not substantially changed in recent years. He located a strain of the TSS staphylococcus in a stock culture that had been collected in Australia in 1928, confirming that the existence of the staph was not new. When he began looking at the composition of tampons, a hypothesis emerged: somehow new ingredients were facilitating the production of TSS toxins. Tierno confirmed this at the time by comparing the bacterium's growth on existing tampons with its lack of growth on surgical cotton.

But because he was one of the few independent researchers receiving no funding from tampon manufacturers, Tierno's results were always disputed. Aside from attacking his credentials, industry-backed experts testifying in toxic shock syndrome lawsuits argued that comparing tampons with wads of cotton was mixing apples and oranges. They said Tierno needed to test synthetic tampons against cotton tampons for accurate results. The problem was that, until recently, there were no all-cotton tampons on the market.

When Tierno learned that two companies, one British and one Canadian, had begun putting out all-cotton tampons, he rushed to conduct tests. With typical scientific understatement, Tierno and Hanna formally presented their conclusion: "The propensity for all-cotton tampons not to amplify TSST-1 in vitro suggests they would lower the risk for tampon-associated TSS."[17]

Almost simultaneously with the publication of Tierno and Hanna's article, New York attorney Martis Ann Brachtl was filing a brief in the U.S. District Court of Kansas on behalf of toxic shock victims. Seeking certification for a class action suit against Tambrands and Playtex, Brachtl asserted that "both defendants have known since 1985 that tampons, which contain highly absorbent fibers, . . . increase the production of Toxic Shock Syndrome." In 1985, after a jury assessed an $11.5

million verdict against Playtex for its reckless disregard in continuing to sell the high-absorbency tampons despite knowing that women had died as a result, both Playtex and Tambrands removed their high-absorbency rayon polyacrylate tampons from the market. Brachtl insists they didn't go far enough. They left their tampons containing highly absorbent viscose rayon on the market, where they remain today.

Playtex countered the lawsuit, claiming that viscose rayon is harmless. "The government and reputable scientific research have not shown any association between the type of tampon fiber and the risk of toxic shock syndrome," said Playtex spokesperson Marty Petersen. "Playtex also believes that the new study by NYU biologists is flawed and not valid." Tambrands agreed, calling the lawsuit "completely and totally without merit." Decrying Tierno's study as "bad research," Tambrands' Bruce Garren said, "He's been saying the same thing for ten years and no one has listened. The FDA didn't listen, Health and Welfare didn't listen, every regulatory body that oversees tampons has approved rayon in tampons—in the face of Tierno's research."

Instead, tampon manufacturers have responded to the continuing presence of toxic shock syndrome by shifting responsibility to the consumer, telling women to change tampons more frequently and to choose the lowest suitable absorbency. How effective has this initiative been? Although there was only one TSS death last year, the number of cases of nonfatal but often serious toxic shock syndrome remains substantial. Extrapolating from FDA figures, Brachtl calculates that between 24,240 and 119,680 American women contracted TSS between 1985 and 1994, though the infamous Rely had long since been pulled from the shelves.

While the toxic shock scandal may not have been entirely preventable, corporate irresponsibility and government apathy certainly contributed to the TSS casualties. Toxic shock sparked a brief flurry of concern in the 1980s that was quickly silenced by an industry skilled in the art of concealment.

Will dioxin get the same treatment? After all, the effects of dioxin are more difficult to monitor and less immediately apparent than those of toxic shock. It may be years before a woman develops any of the symptoms of dioxin poisoning, and because of the level of dioxin in the environment, it would be difficult to point to tampons as contributing to her illness. Sadly, product liability cases are one of the few ways ordinary women can strong-arm corporations into upgrading the safety of their products. While toxic shock lawsuits have informed tampon manufacturers' behavior, the problem of dioxin is more complicated, more subtle, and may ultimately prove more insidious.

Taking a lesson from the congressional tobacco hearings, I suggested to Tierno that the personal product was political and asked him whether he envisioned a similar independent investigation into tampons. He was not optimistic. "Who is going to give money to do research on tampons? The government?" Tierno doubted it. "Frankly speaking, this is not a priority issue." And the industry likes it that way. As Tierno's favorite Rely ad put it: "Let us absorb the worry."

TARGETED MARKETING:
THE STEALTH CAMPAIGN

In most ways, the menstrual products industry is like any other. It plays on women's insecurities—Am I leaking? Will this pad show?—and develops ad campaigns to maximize these fears. Where it departs from mainstream corporate culture is in the secrecy that permeates every aspect of the business. Promising the invisibility of its products, it carries that commitment into its factories and boardrooms, cultivating a low profile that precludes public scrutiny.

Consider Rutland, Vermont, a Tambrands factory town for more than fifty years. When I searched for the large plant, which operates around the clock, it was nearly impossible to find. No road signs announced the location of the powder-blue factory. No mementos of corporate sponsorship or donations were prominently displayed in parks or community centers. There was no hint of the company's presence in local lore. Proudly displayed in the "Vermont Room" of the Rutland Public Library were old ledgers from Vermont Marble; reports and minutes from meetings of the Vermont Dairymen's Association; books on Vermont surgeons, Vermont cheesemaking, local logging, bees, and wildflowers. Though Tambrands had been in Rutland since 1943, the well-intentioned volunteers at the Rutland Historical Society could unearth only a single slim file on it. Inside were three aerial photographs and one promotional shot. There were none of the ephemera or anecdotes that tend to collect in such places. No mention of how Tampax factories produced bandages during World War II; of how the inventor of the modern tampon and double-tubed applicator also invented the flexible ring for the diaphragm; of how the first Tampax salesman used to introduce his product to druggists by asking for a drink of water, then dropping a tampon into the water, then talking about its absorbency and finally, its use. What did I expect? A factory outlet selling seconds? A menstrual products diorama in Rutland's airport? Not exactly. Just a nod to the industry's impact on the local economy. A cordial tour of the plant and some sign that this company, long an integral part of the community, existed. Not only were tampons completely absent from the annals of civic pride but, according to one employee, until three years earlier there hadn't even been a sign in front of the factory to acknowledge its presence.

Since I was denied a tour, all I would see of this Tambrands plant was its reception area, dominated by the company's framed Mission Statement. Full of noble phrasing, the management commits itself to excellence and concludes with the pledge "Our motto will be, 'If it isn't broke, fix it anyway.'"

The slogan's an apt one. Consider this: since the dawn of Kotex, advertisements for disposable pads have been full of dire warnings about odor. For example, one 1920s scenario shows a "dean of women" discussing modern hygiene and odor with a troubled student. "Many women are unconsciously guilty. At certain times they are seriously offensive to others. With realization comes constant fear." Fast-forward fifty years and Playtex plays on the same insecurities. "The nice thing about a tampon is it keeps you odor-free. Or does it?" This 1972 double-page spread depicts an anxious woman alone at a party, a swirl of revelers in the background. Playtex assures this lonely pariah that its tampon "reduces any doubt about intimate odor, but in a very gentle, totally feminine way that's very reassuring." And suddenly Tampax too, which has averred since its very first ad in 1936—and in just about every ad for decades afterward—that "Tampax eliminates odor because it prevents its formation," has begun to push perfumed tampons.

"You're right in pointing out that there may be a definitional problem," conceded Tambrands' Bruce Garren, though he couldn't recall the "odor-free" plug being a standard pitch. "Still, there is a body of consumers who believe there may be an odor . . . and we want to give our consumer what she wants."

In 1996, Tambrands was peddling the same logic about the 100-percent-cotton tampons it introduced. With different motivation. Instead of creating need where there is none, they were creating products and denying they were needed. "There was no medical reasoning," Janey Loyd, vice president of business development for Tambrands told the New York *Daily News* at the time. "Our decision was based on a segment of consumers who consistently told us they wanted all-natural product protection. These are the same women who like all-natural foods and wear cotton clothing."[18] (In fact, a small all-cotton-tampon manufacturer, Natracare, filed a suit against Tambrands in 1997, alleging that the interior of the tampon might be cotton but that the overwrap, or sheath of webbing that binds the tampon, was not. Therefore, Natracare said, Tambrands was engaging in false advertisement. Tambrands refuted this, and the case is pending.) What Tambrands saw in the emerging hippy-dippy, organic food, all-natural-fibers cadre was a marketing opportunity. If people will pay more for organic food, then it stood to make a bundle with all-cotton tampons. Without in any way admitting that its predominantly rayon products might contain dioxin or contribute to toxic shock, Tambrands began offering women an alternative—at a price. While regular tampons cost about $3.50 for a box of eighteen, Naturals retail for about $3.90 for a box of sixteen.

Of course, it's not news to suggest that sanitary protection companies, like the rest of corporate America, will go to great lengths to grow their profits. But when the prices of other staples—like milk, or wheat, or even the Florida orange crop—fluctuate, a national debate ensues. Economists, experts, and financial analysts all weigh in with advice for Uncle Sam and consumers. The government even intervenes with regulations or subsidies from time to time. But so what if nearly half the population feels the pinch when sanitary protection prices rise? So what if bleeding is a billion-dollar business? The evening news isn't likely to comment on price increases, just as we aren't likely to extol brand virtues over cocktails, or even comparison-shop in the supermarket. In a way, why bother?

At most drugstores, a box of forty o.b.'s may cost 8 percent less than a 46-pack of Tampax, but the six extra tampons you get with the Tampax package make the price differential insignificant. Each brand of tampon seems pegged to the cost of its neighbor. And the 1990s have seen a rapid increase in the price of tampons, with a corresponding decrease in the number of tampons per box. In fact, Tambrands bragged to shareholders in 1991 that "we made product and packaging improvements, reduced the size and price of our packages, and increased our price per tampon." What the consumer saw that year was the same basic product with a new "tamper-evident" seal and a slightly altered applicator—the "comfort-shaped" tip is rounded—while the number of sticks in a box decreased from forty to thirty-two. As if that weren't bad enough, in 1992 Tambrands and Playtex came out with a box containing even fewer tampons. Again, Tambrands told its shareholders: "We have announced a new package size in the United States, a 20-count that will retail at the most attractive price point for feminine protection products while further increasing our realization per tampon." (PaineWebber financial analyst Andrew Shore estimated that Tambrands was raking in at least $1.21 in profit per box of 32, and slightly more than that with the 20-count boxes.) By 1998, Tambrands had reduced the 32-pack to a 30-pack and the 20-pack to an 18-pack.

At the same time, industry giants spent the 1990s duking it out for a larger share of a finite market. As the baby boomers enter menopause, the manufacturers are fighting over a *shrinking* market by scrambling to lure customers with new products and by setting their sights on developing nations, where many women still use homemade pads. (Adorned with a lovely soft-focus photo of an Asian woman—with insets of an egg, then an ugly duckling, and finally a swan—a Tambrands annual report drools over China, where "a menstruating population of 335 million women, plus an economy experiencing explosive growth, define an exceptionally promising market for Tambrands.")

Inventiveness—though hardly genuine innovation—reigns. In the last decade we have seen a host of new products. Kotex has introduced curved pads. Kimberly-Clark has introduced pads with "StayPut" tabs. Procter & Gamble has introduced its Whisper line (Shhh, our secret) and its Always with "wings and quilted sides." Playtex has introduced Silk Glides (cardboard applicators with a glossy coat). Tambrands has introduced Tampax Satin Touch (same thing), Tampax Lites (described by an employee as "the old juniors"), and the

Tampax Multi-Pack (twelve "supers," fourteen "regulars," and four "lites"; a marketing concept that generalizes a woman's flow into a tidy uniformity of need). Johnson & Johnson, maker of the nonapplicator o.b., has added the "comfort design applicator." And Stayfree pads now come with "Four Wall Protection"—whatever that means. And of course there's the new packaging to make women think there's an upgraded product inside. Old products, new products, old products dressed as new products—all things considered, we're talking about a $1.7 billion feminine hygiene industry.

To nurture and replenish their market, the sanitary protection industry has a long tradition of hawking to pubescents. "One fundamental truth drives our business from Chicago to Shanghai: the consumer we attract today will likely stay with us for all the years of her menstrual cycle," Martin Emmett, chair and CEO of Tambrands, told shareholders in 1993. "If we can persuade young women to use our product during their early teens, we can gain loyal consumers for thirty-five years or more."

Sending representatives into schools and classrooms across the country, Tambrands bragged in 1991 that it reached 20 percent of the 1.8 million thirteen-year-old girls in the United States and 21 percent of the same group in Canada. Their educational program, a kind of traveling menstrual show, includes a teaching kit—replete with Tampax product samples, of course. To make things easier on the tongue-tied teacher who'd rather not say the M-word, there's a video called *Kids to Kids: Talking About Puberty*, which contains teen testimonials of girls who remind one another that you can't lose your virginity from tampons, that you can't get them into the wrong hole, and that, unlike pads, with tampons "there's no possible odor." Students also learn that, while you may start out with pads, "after a while you start to kind of shift over to tampons." There are lots of girlish giggles and red faces, but girls soon discover "how to find the right feminine protection without even blushing."

Put out by Lifetime Learning Systems, Inc., which also provides "accurate," "factual," and "objective" educational material for other pulp and paper industries (my personal favorite is a coloring book put out by the logging industry featuring Timbear, a fuzzy grizzly who cuts down trees because he understands the importance of "controlled growth" in the environment), the package peddles Tampax quite shamelessly. For example, one quiz lays out ten hypothetical situations, such as "I have a swim meet at the YWCA on Saturday" or "I don't want to risk having odor" or "I have new white shorts and my period just started. How can I be sure I am protected?" Students are presumably graded on the correct answer: tampon, pad, or panty shield.

Soon, though, even girls who incorrectly choose "pad" as their answer may be acing the test. In July 1997, Procter & Gamble, makers of Always pads, bought the tampon all-star, Tambrands, for $1.85 billion, more than P&G had ever spent on a purchase. (With the new merger, "puberty education" material can now make product recommendations across the board, referring girls to Secret deodorant, a P&G product, in a lesson on body odor and suggesting Cheer, another P&G product, to get those stubborn bloodstains off her panties — the ones she incurred using a competitor's inadequate product, of course! And extra credit for the overachieving student who declares a pad-plug combo her answer to a leak-free life.) With news of the acquisition, shares in both Tambrands and P&G stock went up; with finalization of the sale, the doors to Tambrands' Palmer, Massachusetts, plant and its White Plains, New York, office were shut and hundreds of workers laid off. Procter & Gamble was consolidating operations at its Cincinnati headquarters and couldn't wait to put its mark on Tampax.

For Procter & Gamble, makers of Rely, its seventeen-year hiatus in tampon-making was finally over. And it stood to make a killing. Not only could it take women from menarche to menopause, but its rayon-and-paper products would swaddle her genitals and collect her bodily effluent from cradle (Pampers, Luvs) to grave (Attends) — and caress her labia every day in between if she was a Charmin user. But while P&G's existing line of pads, Always and Whisper, already dominated the napkin market, with 36 percent of the sales, and Tambrands carried nearly 50 percent of the tampon market,[19] the U.S. Justice Department's antitrust regulators ruled that the P&G-Tambrands merger did not give Procter an unfair competitive advantage in the feminine hygiene field. In the Justice Department's mind, pad-users and tampon-users were separate sets of consumers and their numbers should not be lumped together. But the logic is skewed. Though 70 percent of American women report using tampons during the day, those numbers drop to 25 percent at night.[20] Assuming women are using *something* at night, it's probably safe to say it's pads. (Indeed, had the United States Justice Department trotted over to the United States Food and Drug Administration, it would have learned that our own government advocates a rotating regime of protection, recommending in a 1993 FDA memo that "tampon use should be alternated with menstrual pad use" to reduce the risk of

TSS.[21]) But the Justice Department, which approved the merger within weeks, didn't spend a whole lot of time agonizing over consumer rights in this case. The winners? P&G. The losers? Women, whose options just got a whole lot narrower.

After all, Procter & Gamble is notoriously ruthless in its pursuit of profit. Now that it has dragged the aging Tambrands into its lair and can apply its vast market muscle, women can expect to see some real changes in the sanitary protection field over the next few years. While P&G's Rely tampon may have been a disaster, the company is betting almost $2 billion that the purchase of Tambrands will restore its credibility. (And there have been a few hints—purchase of a patent, reference to Tambrands as "a strong brand we can bring technology to"[22]—that P&G has a new tampon coming.) As P&G's history has indicated, it gobbles up competitors with some strategic goals in mind.

Procter & Gamble, founded in 1837 by immigrants William Procter and James Gamble, who converted hog fat from Cincinnati's huge meat-packing industry into tallow for soap and candles, has gone on to develop or acquire more than 300 products, which it sells in 140 countries today. With $35 billion in revenue in 1997, P&G is the eighteenth-largest corporation in the United States. From its trademark Ivory soap to its Tide, Prell, Pampers, and Pringles, P&G is everywhere— quite literally—with its products found in 98 percent of U.S. households.[23] The company boasts that it sells $60 worth of P&G products for every man, woman, and child in the United States.[24] And when it comes to international sales, P&G sold enough products in 1997 to reap the equivalent of $6.30 from each person on the planet.

If P&G has its way, those numbers are about to go up. Way up. CEO John Pepper recently announced to financial analysts that he intended to increase sales by $10 billion over the next ten years. What was going to help catapult him to his goal? The company's brand-new menstrual products monopoly. Pepper explained that he will be working Tambrands hard, intending to double its current yearly sales of $662 million over the next decade.[25]

Procter & Gamble also sees tremendous global expansion potential for tampons. While 70 percent of American women use tampons, only 100 million of the world's 1.7 billion menstruating women do.[26] In Asia and Latin America, two of the most populous parts of the world, only 3 percent of all women use tampons. P&G is gearing up for a major campaign to persuade women with a "cultural bias" against tampon use to change their ways. With a mass-marketing campaign, P&G hopes to lure women away from a tradition of homemade cloth pads. Women will learn to use disposable pads or tampons; it's a win-win situation for Procter. "We're always looking for the core benefit areas we can advertise [in] . . . and modify culturally," Pepper told the *Cincinnati Enquirer* in April 1997, describing a new "educational" campaign. Presenting his company as a harbinger of progress and enlightenment, Pepper explained that P&G executives were sensitive to local custom. "The starting point always in our company is to go in and understand the consumer where they are now."[27]

When it comes to the American consumer, P&G is counting on her complacency—and embarrassment—to keep her from asking too many questions. As long as women are kept ignorant of the makeup of tampons and pads—what kinds of perfumes, surfactants, and materials go into a product—and don't worry about the cumulative impact of harmful materials in earlier-generation tampons (with higher levels of dioxin), contemporary ones (with lower levels), and even all-cotton ones (which come from crops regularly dusted with pesticides), P&G can continue on its way unhindered. Certainly no federal agency such as the FDA is likely to push for more stringent standards without consumer pressure. Today, P&G echoes the line that served Tambrands so well, assuring women that there are no health risks associated with its products. "We don't have detectable levels of dioxin," says P&G spokesperson Elaine Plummer, explaining that its rayon suppliers use the new EPA-mandated chlorine dioxide process. "This has been shown to virtually eliminate potential formation of dioxin during the bleaching of fibers." Clearly, P&G is purchasing a new reputation with its Tambrands acquisition—and rewriting history. "Tampax has a heritage of safe, trusted performance and, like all of P&G's paper products, it is designed, packaged, and labeled so that it can be safely and confidently used by our consumers."

Certain that P&G's 1980 debacle with Rely and toxic shock syndrome won't hinder tampon sales today, CEO John Pepper declared P&G innocent of wrongdoing in the TSS scandal. "Enough time has passed now where that record is very clear," he told the *Cincinnati Enquirer* in April 1997.[28] What he is actually banking on is that enough time has passed for women to have forgotten about Rely. If it once prematurely rushed a product to the shelves without adequate safety testing, so what? That was almost twenty years ago.

Those in the business community agree. This is an act of financial daring and foresight. Pepper's business acumen will make his stockholders rich. An April 1997 story in *Marketing Week* summed things up nicely:

> P&G's corporate image was badly tarnished [with Rely].
> It emerged from the affair looking like a reckless corporate bully that put profit before the lives of its customers.
> But consumers' memories are notoriously short, and few remember the details of the debacle in the U.S., let alone in other parts of the world.[29]

So far, the prediction has held up. To date, coverage of Procter & Gamble's purchase of Tambrands—though the biggest in P&G's history—was mostly limited to the business pages, and the company has successfully kept news of the merger quiet.

PART TWO

The Adolescent

HOW COULD YOU DO THIS TO ME, MOM?! DID YOU THINK I'D HAVE TO FLOAT TO SCHOOL? DID YOU THINK IT WOULD DOUBLE AS AN AIRBAG IF THE SCHOOL BUS GOT INTO AN ACCIDENT? WHY DON'T YOU JUST PIN A SCARLET "P" ON MY CHEST? OR HAVE THE PRINCIPAL MAKE AN ANNOUNCEMENT THAT DIANE FIELDS HAS HER PERIOD TODAY?! I'M SORRY, BUT I'M NOT GONNA WADDLE AROUND ALL DAY WEARING THESE SUPERSIZED PADS. WRITE ME A NOTE. I'M SICK TODAY.
LEADING REGULAR
ALWAYS ULTRA
DIANE WOULDN'T BE HAVING SUCH A COW IF SHE KNEW ABOUT ALWAYS ULTRA®. THEY'RE ULTRA THIN PADS WITH A SUPER-ABSORBENT CORE THAT TRAPS MOISTURE BETTER THAN HER MOM'S REGULAR HOMECOMING FLOAT PADS⁺. BUT STAY CLEANER AND DRIER THANKS TO DRI-WEAVE – THE TINY FUNNELS ON TOP OF THE PAD THAT HELP PULL WETNESS AWAY FROM THE SURFACE AND KEEP IT AWAY. THEN DIANE COULD SAVE THE GUILT TRIP – AND THE SICK NOTE – FOR ANOTHER DAY.
IT'S CLEANER. IT'S DRIER. IT'S ALWAYS.
⁺vs. leading competitive regular non-wing maxis © P&G1997
www.always.com

n a warm Saturday in July, I sit beneath a shady tree talking with five giggling nine- and ten-year-olds. I'm spending the weekend at a girls' summer camp in the Catskills, where I'm interviewing campers, aged nine to fifteen, about menstruation. These girls, the youngest of the bunch, have not gotten their periods yet; all are curious about it. The girls trade information and misinformation and worry that their periods will arrive before they've got the facts down. Their knowledge of the facts is indeed sketchy, but their grasp of the message—Shhhh!—is profound.

"Let's talk about menstruation," I begin.

"Which means 'period,'" a ten-year-old translates for her chums. She knows because she just learned the word over lunch yesterday, when the camp director announced that a woman who was writing a book about menstruation would be visiting and did anyone want to sign up to talk to her? Rebecca Rose, who will be entering fifth grade in the fall and who, like all the girls I interviewed, chose her own pseudonym, is delighted to have been granted permission to bandy the term about. "Period! Period!" she says, in a singsong chant. There's something naughty, she's sure, about saying the word aloud.

Her best friend, ten-year-old Rosie Marie (there was a bit of an argument over who owned the coveted name Rose), says that she knows what menstruation is: "It's a thing your mom gets and gets really cranky and says, 'Back off.'"

"It's bad," Rebecca Rose says, then drops her voice to whisper, "Bloody."

"Oh, gross! You said that word!" Rosie Marie shouts.

"Blood," Rebecca repeats timidly. She brushes her cropped blond bangs off her forehead and looks straight at Rosie. She gets defiant. "Blood," she repeats.

Rebecca turns back to me. "My mom said it's bloody. My mom got a book out of the library once and showed me."

"I got a book, *What's Happening to Me?*" interjects a ten-year-old. A plump child with dark, curly hair and olive skin, this fifth-grader would like to be called Anonymous. We settle on Missy for short. Missy is clearly the most well-read of the group. She is a serious and curious child who has already discovered she'll find more complete answers to her questions about menstruation (and sex) in books than from grown-ups. "I found the book at my grandparents' on the bookshelf," she tells me. Clearly, Missy lapped it up, committing whole sections to memory. She sits up straight and recites for me the section on menstruation: "It said, 'It's more of a chore than a pleasure.'"

I'm intrigued. "What is menstruation, exactly?" I ask the girls.

"Blood!" Rosie shouts. Then she smiles guiltily at me, waiting for a reprimand. When none comes, she nudges Rebecca. "Blood," she says again.

But Rebecca doesn't answer. She's conflicted. This topic is steep competition for her attention. She's got lots of questions. Maybe some of them will get answered. "What is periods?" she repeats. She turns away from Rosie, trying to concentrate. "Periods come from . . ." She pauses. She's not sure where they come from or why.

"It's so you can have kids," Rosie says.

"If you don't use one of your eggs, it just comes out in your period," Missy explains.

The other two girls in the group have been silent until this point. When I look at nine-year-old Sandra, a beautiful, self-possessed Hispanic child, to see if she has anything to say, she tells me that her mom talked to her about periods. "She told me that it comes from . . ." Points to crotch. "There." Sandra shrugs. "That's all she told me."

"No one told me," Rosie interjects. She pushes strands of stringy hair off her sweaty face. "No one."

"I told you," Rebecca corrects. "I told the whole cabin last night! You bleed."

"At school they don't talk about it until the fifth grade," Missy laments.

"They don't tell us anything at my school. Nothing," Rebecca says. "Well, nothing gross like that."

"In *Are You There God? It's Me, Margaret* there's a woman who came to their school and showed them a video about it, and she called it *menooostration*," Missy says, quoting, quite accurately, from the book she later admits she's read five times.

Finally Laura waves her hand to be called on. A heavyset ten-year-old wearing an oversized T-shirt and stretch pants, Laura has held back, not sure what she can contribute to the conversation. But suddenly she's got a story to tell. Her *secret caché*? She's seen "The Movie." All eyes are on her. "We saw the films at school. We were watching them, and . . . well, the boys didn't see our movie because . . ."

"Wait till we get to the fifth grade, Rosie!" Rebecca says. "I wouldn't mind if we talked about it in front of boys as long as I know more what it is."

Laura ignores her. "It was a title like *A Lady to a Girl.* Or something like that."

"How do you know when you're going to get it?" Rebecca interrupts.

"*Girl to a Woman.* It's called *Girl to a Woman*, not *Lady to a Girl*," Missy corrects. "I saw it in *Harriet the Spy*."

"How do you know," Rebecca says again, "when you're going to get it?"

"In the movie, it showed the changes you go through," Laura continues. "And it was about a girl who did have it." Laura lowers her voice and goes into a long story about a girl who went to the store to buy pads but her brother saw her dad giving her money and wanted to know why *she* got money and he didn't, and then when they were in the store her brother snatched the pads out of her hands and they fell on the floor and everybody was looking at them. "It was terrible. It was so embarrassing."

"What? What was terrible? To buy them?" Rebecca wants to know.

No one answers her.

"I have a question," Rebecca says again. "When do you get your period?"

"It just happens one day," Rosie says, impatiently. "It mostly happens at night."

"In *Are You There God?* Margaret's aunt didn't get it until she was sixteen," Missy says.

"Is there a certain age you get it, though?" Rebecca says again.

Missy finally answers her. "Around eleven or twelve."

Ten-year-old Rebecca sighs with relief. "So I have time."

THE PLUMMETING AGE OF PUBERTY
AND THE "EPIDEMIC" OF TEEN SEX

While the girls at camp worry about the nitty-gritty details of menarche—When is it going to happen to me and what will it feel like when it does?—health-policy experts and the press put a more ominous spin on the event: the onset of menstruation means the onset of sex, and teen sex means teen pregnancy, and teen moms mean skyrocketing welfare costs.

This logic forms the subtext for dozens of policy discussions about "the teen pregnancy problem" and has as its origin a 1976 study reporting that the age of menarche (the onset of menstruation) was falling dramatically among Americans. While the average age of menarche in the United States today is approximately twelve and a half, J. M. Tanner, an authority on physical development, noted that in the early 1800s, the average age at the onset of menstruation was seventeen. Owing to better nutrition, he speculated, girls today are maturing much earlier. According to Tanner, the age at menarche has been dropping by four months per decade. The report, hardly groundbreaking, would probably have slipped quietly into academic obscurity except that it happened to coincide with a rash of inflammatory rhetoric about adolescent promiscuity and a teen pregnancy epidemic.

Although a link between early menstruation and early sexual activity has never been conclusively established, Tanner's modest report about the plummeting age of puberty hit a nerve. As Vern Bullough noted in a 1983 essay, Tanner's "early menarche" theory, while of questionable accuracy, quickly became the jumping-off point for a new round of hysteria about sexually precocious girls.[1] Beginning in 1976, the media latched onto the theory and spun dozens of alarmist stories. *Newsweek, Time,* and *The Nation* all wrote about Tanner's findings, asking what we were to do with this nation of sexually precocious girls. In the ensuing years, the press recycled the story with predictable regularity.

Take *Newsweek*. In September of 1980, the magazine ran a story titled "The Games Teen-Agers Play," using Tanner's study as a premise to warn that "something has happened to those endearing young charmers who used to wobble around playing grownup in Mom's high heels." With a predictable swipe at working moms, reporters explained that kids "are reaching puberty earlier, finding new freedom from parental restraints, taking cues from a pleasure-bent culture and playing precocious sex games in the bedroom—often while Mom and Dad are at work." The danger was not randy boys, but Lolita girls. "For adolescent boys, sex has always been regarded as a rite of passage, like getting permission to drive the family car," reporter David Gelman wrote. It appears to have recently become "a ceremonial of young womanhood as well." Bemoaning "sexual adventurism among young girls," the teen pregnancy "epidemic," and the "rampant" venereal disease resulting from this "carnal knowledge," Gelman used the Tanner study as a springboard to launch into a diatribe about girls whose "sexual awareness thus runs breathlessly ahead of their emotional development." Full of euphemisms for sex, like "stampeding into sin," "going over the brink," and "unseemly sexual stirrings," *Newsweek* fanned the flames of "precocious puberty" alarmism, roundly condemning this new breed of copulating schoolgirl.

Who's to blame? The article faults feminism ("Taking a misread leaf from women's lib, [girls] are becoming sexually aggressive and strutting a kind of locker-room swagger about their conquests"), absentee moms ("The vast increase of working mothers has provided a convenient sexual setting: according to some researchers, the empty house after school has become the favorite trysting spot"), and, of course—the requisite mea culpa—the media ("Sexual precocity is being packaged and promoted—and taken as the norm—throughout the popular culture"). It's not just that the "tender young things are sampling sex before its season," it's that *boys* are being "harassed" by "the newly demanding girls."

Fast-forward a decade and *Newsweek* runs the same story. As news. This time, the magazine calls it "The End of Innocence" and places it in the May 1991 special issue on kids. Again, Tanner's study on the declining age of menarche becomes the basis for a warning that kids in the 1990s are, sexually speaking, "two to three years ahead of their counterparts a quarter of a century ago." Since presumably the sexually active teens the magazine was excoriating a decade ago are the parents of today's young children, the authors of "The End of Innocence" up the ante a bit by suggesting that vigilance needs to begin even sooner—with toddlers. "The sexual acceleration starts early and holds throughout adolescence," they write. "A 3-year-old who no longer holds her mother's hand becomes a 6-year-old more interested in MTV than Bambi and a 9-year-old who can discuss homosexuality, AIDS and transsexual surgery." The article continues to blame the media (this time *Geraldo*, the previous year's blockbuster movie *Pretty Woman*, and the pop song "Me So Horny" take hits) and moms ("Most mothers aren't home when their kids return from school and can't exert day-to-day control").

Clearly, a decline in the average age at menarche, while neither as radical nor as insidious in origin as it is generally portrayed, would influence contemporary views about teen sex. But how accurate is it?

Tanner's statistics, and the leaps in logic they spawned, may be suspect. Despite references to an "epidemic" of teen births, the rate of teen births in the United States has actually dropped in the past few decades. According to the National Center for Health Statistics, the rate has declined from 525,000 teen births in 1956 to 513,000 in 1995.[2] While *any* births to girls who aren't ready to be mothers is problematic, it's important to put the "crisis" in context: what has changed since the 1950s is not that more girls are having babies, it's that more girls are having babies out of wedlock. Those numbers have shot up, so that while only 15 percent of teenage girls who gave birth in 1960 were unmarried, 75 percent were unmarried in 1994.[3] In other words, the number of shotgun weddings has declined.

Still, one could argue that even if slightly fewer girls are having babies now, that's due to birth control and abortion, not to lack of sex. Certainly more teens are sexually active today—nearly 70 percent by the time they're seventeen, reports the Alan Guttmacher Institute[4]—and that has everybody—politicians, policy experts, parents, and preachers—up in arms. "Puberty" is a code word for sexual activity, and if the age of puberty is declining, the reasoning goes, then we're all in trouble.

Tanner's 1976 study on the declining age of menarche has been called into question by a number of researchers. Bullough's well-reasoned critique suggests that Tanner inappropriately mixed data, relying heavily on a Norwegian study from 1884 that reported the average onset of menstruation at age seventeen, to the exclusion of other European sources that put it closer to fourteen or fifteen.[5] The age of menstruation *has* dropped somewhat. But most contemporary researchers describe a more gradual decline, from an average age of fifteen to an average age of twelve and a half, attributing the change to improvements in nutrition.[6] Indeed, in some developing countries where nutrition is considerably poorer, menstruation still occurs later.

Experts put forward two different theories about why nutrition has an impact on menarche. Some believe that menstruation begins when a girl's bones reach a critical mass, that is, when her pelvic bones are mature enough to accommodate pregnancy and birth. Others insist that it has more to do with body fat. "You don't mature, or menstruate, until you have the right body composition and fat, which translate into energy for reproduction," claims Rose Frisch, an associate professor of population sciences at the Harvard School of Public Health. After doing comparative studies on adolescent dancers, a notoriously lean class of girls, Frisch discovered that they start menstruation later than their peers. She hypothesized that this was due to a lack of body fat. Scientists have recently lent further credence to this theory by testing it out with mice. Using a synthetic fat hormone called Leptin, they fooled prepubescent mice into thinking their bodies were fatter than they were. The rodents were quickly propelled into puberty.[7]

While some theories about the declining age of menarche, like the fat-and-nutrition one, seem logical, other explanations seem downright bizarre—and all are given equal credence by the press. For example, in July 1991, *The New York Times* ran an article linking early puberty to childhood stress. Citing Tanner's figures on the declining age of menarche, the article recounts a new theory: girls are menstruating sooner as a survival tactic. Dr. Jay Belsky, a psychologist at Pennsylvania State University and an influential figure in the anti-day-care movement who has equally extreme views on the dangers of day care to children's development, had focused public attention on the subject by speculating that girls who grow up in stressful conditions—which he defines as living with single mothers in inner cities—have their periods sooner than other girls because they are subconsciously practicing a new reproductive strategy. "Children who grow up in dangerous conditions, [Belsky's] theory holds, are primed to boost the chances of having their genes survive into the next generation by choosing earlier sex, earlier motherhood, and more children," the *Times* summarizes.[8]

Belsky marshals several studies in defense of his argument. One, published by Dr. Michele Surbey, studied 1,123 girls in Toronto and reported that those who had grown up in homes where their parents were fighting and then divorced reached puberty four months earlier than the control group. Another, which looked at 501 girls in New Zealand, discovered that the longer a girl's father was absent, the earlier the girl menstruated. Assuming a link between early menstruation and early sex, Belsky told the *Times*: "When a child learns that the world is insecure and risky, the biological response is to get into reproduction sooner. Because the danger is that if you don't, you won't reproduce at all." But critics like Dr. Terrie Moffit, who co-authored the New Zealand study, put a different spin on the statistics. Because girls tend to get their first periods at roughly the same age their mothers did, Moffit speculates that these early menstruaters come from families where the mother got her period early and was propelled prematurely into adulthood. Maybe she got married earlier, made a bad decision, and got divorced sooner. Though controversial, Belsky's theories are taken seriously by the scientific establishment: in the fall of 1991, the respected journal *Child Development* published his paper on this topic.

Other theories linking early menstruation and sexual precocity abound. Dr. Rose Frisch, widely known for her aforementioned studies of adolescent dancers and menstruation, once responded to a query from an aide in Senator Daniel Patrick Moynihan's office. "He [the aide] asked if it was true that more jazzy environments or exposure to sexy stuff makes girls have their periods sooner," she said. Frisch assured him that even studies dating back to the Victorian era that compared "bawdy" servant girls (who were hit on by their male employers and generally had more access to information about sex) to their coddled and protected mistresses showed that it was nutrition, not sex, that affected the timing of menarche: the servants reached menarche *after* their mistresses did. For Frisch, Moynihan's aide's question and Belsky's theory are one and the same, both part of a general trend to view the onset of menstruation as linked to ominous social trends. "There's so much junk out there about what causes menstruation," she says. "I'm constantly amazed."

But the "junk" is revealing. There are those, like Belsky (and his like-minded comrades at *Newsweek* who find sexuality in young girls a terrifying concept) who believe menstruating makes girls more sexually active. And there are those, like the

Moynihan aide, who believe girls' exposure to sex makes them menstruate earlier. The fact that people approach the issue from both sides underlines how intertwined child sexuality and menstruation are in people's minds. No matter where girls glean information about periods—the formal curriculum (menstrual-ed tracts), the informal curriculum (teen magazines), or menstrual classics (Judy Blume's *Are You There God? It's Me, Margaret*, Steven King's *Carrie*, Anne Frank's diary)—they learn that menstruation and sex are inextricably linked.

SEX AND THE MENSTRUAL GENRE

Americans have a long and shrill history of fretting over sexual precocity in girls. In 1910 a Dr. B. S. Talmey wrote in *Genesis: A Manual for the Instruction of Children in Matters Sexual* that "the average child in the city today, between the ages of ten and fifteen, knows things that would make their parents' hair stand on end, if they supposed for one moment that their child is conversant with such matters."[9] Even progressives like Dr. William J. Robinson, who was a pioneering advocate for birth control and convinced the president of the American Medical Association to publicly endorse contraception in 1912,[10] warned about modern girls and their new "sexual immorality" as early as 1917. "The increase in sexual freedom or licentiousness during the past twenty years has been greater than in the preceding two hundred," he wrote in *Woman: Her Sex and Love Life*. The book, a best-seller that was reissued five times, claimed that virginal girls were "the exception, not the rule" and described a dangerous new trend:

Many young girls, barely out of their teens, consider sexual intercourse of no more importance or significance than touching hands or lips was considered by their sisters of a generation ago.[11]

What *has* changed about these warnings is that at the turn of the century and up until the 1940s, they were used to persuade middle-class parents that they desperately needed to teach their daughters the facts of life if they were to prevent them from sexual experimentation. Today, of course, similar diatribes imply that young girls know *too much* for their own good.

Obviously, authors of sex-education books tend to favor frank discussions; otherwise they wouldn't be in the sex-ed business. But in prefaces and introductions from as long ago as 1850 to as recently as 1997, sex-ed authors suggest that existing material is inadequate, laud a brave new menstrual glasnost, present themselves as harbingers of the modern word, and then regurgitate the same old stuff. The text is presented as enlightened, the authors as daring, the subject itself as original. The anecdote of choice, trotted out with predictable regularity, cites a daughter or niece or cousin on the precipice of puberty. The benevolent author searches the stacks at libraries and bookstores for appropriate educational material and finds nothing. She or he rectifies the situation by writing a book.[12]

Some of these early books, like *The Married Woman's Private Medical Companion*, written by Dr. A. M. Mauriceau in 1854,[13] were clearly written for adult women and were more the exception, in that era, than the rule. But by the turn of the century, the rise of an expert class (doctors, researchers, scientists), the popular interpretation of germ theory, the social hygiene movement, and the Progressive movement led to dozens of didactic pamphlets and self-help books sermonizing about why mothers should tell their daughters about menstruation and why they should tell them about it *this* way. By the 1920s, the Girl Scouts even had a menstruation badge, discreetly called the Health Winner Badge. Teens earned this badge by learning the correct terms for women's reproductive organs, having a one-on-one chat about the topic with their leader, and keeping their leader apprised of their cycles so that she could appropriately monitor—and presumably limit— their physical activities. What is remarkable about reading these texts is not how quaintly archaic they are, but how in line with contemporary thinking they remain.

FORMAL LESSONS: THE ABC'S OF BLOOD

A specific script dominates the menstrual genre. And it's not just the facts—most girls begin menstruating between the ages of twelve and seventeen; girls' periods will be irregular for a year or more after they start menstruating; eventually most will menstruate every twenty-eight days or so; etc.—that are the obvious constants. But the script is presented within clearly defined parameters that have not deviated much in a hundred years. The same format, structure, and themes come up again and again, the only difference being that the more overt classist, racist, and sexist motifs eventually move underground, relegated to the subtext of modern menstrual lit.

The medium may have changed—by the 1950s girls were watching movies as well as reading pamphlets in school—but the message remains the same. One typical instructional film, situated in the middle of the century we're discussing, seems to hit all the bases, but is significant because it also marks a turning point. *Molly Grows Up*, produced in 1953, is a typical dramatization of puberty that was shown in classrooms across the country. But, for the first time, the nitty-gritty details of sanitary protection get big play. Not surprisingly, Molly's menarche is brought to you by the Personal Products Corporation.

Beginning in the 1950s, all of the major manufacturers of sanitary protection began establishing education departments and generating voluminous amounts of instructional material to distribute in schools and drugstores, and via free offers in teen magazines. Recognizing adolescence as a critical developmental juncture—the onset of brand loyalty—these manufacturers naturally sang the praises of their own products in their educational material. Sample products for each student were, of course, included in the teaching kits sent out to schools. The industry put its own spin on periods, pedaling a new, scientific micromanagement of blood. Beginning in the early 1950s with films like *Molly Grows Up*, the menstrual products companies slowly muscled their way into the public schools, where their menstrual education kits have become a staple of modern puberty education.

Molly Grows Up is a menstrual classic. The black-and-white film opens with twelve-year-old Molly describing a wedding to two elderly neighbor ladies. Molly has stars in her eyes. "And golly! You should've seen the bride!" she says, telling the women that the bride wore "the most beautiful dress I've ever seen." Before Molly can elaborate, her best friend calls out to her. Excusing herself, Molly skips off gaily down her suburban sidewalk.

Later in the afternoon, we see Molly preening in the mirror, trying on her sister Jeanie's lipstick and hat. Jeanie catches her and is miffed, but smiles indulgently when the stars return to Molly's eyes. This time Molly is yearning for an event somewhat nearer fruition than marriage: she is caressing a sanitary pad she spies in Jeanie's drawer. (Conveniently, viewers see the brand name—Modess, made by Personal Products Corporation.) "Jeanie, when do you think I'll start having periods, too?" Molly asks. Smiling beatifically from the other side of womanhood, Jeanie assures her, "From the way you've been acting lately, it shouldn't be long now."

Sure enough, Molly comes home from school a few days later with news for Mom, who is in the kitchen baking muffins. "Mom, guess what? I started my first period," Molly says, excited. "Well, what do you know," Mom says, wiping her hands on her apron and pulling up a chair. "Come on, sit down and tell me all about it." Mom's sympathetic: "Well, my goodness, how do you feel?" Mom's prepared with advice: "I'll tell you what. Tonight will be mother-and-daughter conference night. And if you help me with dinner, we'll get to it that much sooner!" Mom's delighted: "Gollllll-y!" she says, stars in *her* eyes, as Molly leaves to wash up.

The next scene is strange, and the only one that even vaguely alludes to sex and the conflicting feelings parents may have about their daughters' budding sexuality. Mom sits in the living room, sewing and talking to Molly about menstruation. Dad—wearing cardigan sweater, holding pipe—comes downstairs, announcing that the fight he was watching is over. "Is this a private conversation?" he asks. Mom says she doesn't think so, and Molly agrees it's not. "Only, *you* tell him," Molly says shyly. Mom stands up for the formal announcement: "Well, Jim, Molly's growing up. She's having her first menstrual period." Dad, busy lighting his pipe, stops abruptly and turns on them. "What?! Already?" Angry and accusatory, he addresses his wife: "For goodness' sake, Alice, I thought . . . I mean, after all, she's only . . ." He pauses, suddenly in the wrong sitcom; wasn't this supposed to be *Father Knows Best?* Molly interrupts. "Oh, Daddy, don't be so silly. I'm not a baby anymore." Annoyed and indignant, he continues, "I know, dear, but . . ." The news has taken him by surprise; the implications are unwelcome. Suddenly he grows silent and gets a faraway look in his eyes. "No, no, honey, I guess you aren't."

In the next scene we see Molly sitting pensively and passively beneath a tree. She twirls a dry leaf while a voice-over tells us the party's over: "Some of the things Molly used to do seem a little silly now. Sometimes she gets all mixed up."

Then we see Molly at school. Sitting in her class—all girls, of course—she listens to the school nurse, Miss Jensen, explain "menstrooo-a-tion." The students get the requisite ram's-head drawing of a uterus on the chalkboard, along with the standard dry information about ovaries, fallopian tubes, uteruses, eggs, and sperm. "If the egg cell unites with the male cell, or sperm, it is fertilized," the nurse tells the girls. There is absolutely no indication of *how* that unification might take place. Or what a "male cell" might be doing free-falling in a girl's uterus. Conveniently, Molly is worried about other things. "Miss Jensen," she asks. "Is it true people can tell when you're menstruating?" she asks. Miss Jensen assures her it's not, then contradicts herself: "But you should be more careful than ever about personal cleanliness and daintiness," she says, implying that slackers will blow their menstrual cover. She tells the girls they should change their underwear more often and "be sure and use a deodorant." She goes on: "And pay more attention to your hair and nails. And plan to wear your prettiest dress. In other words, be your most attractive self."

Because this is sponsored by Personal Products Corporation, Miss Jensen then pulls out a giant Modess pad and, to indicate how it would be used, nestles it next to the sketch of a girl's figure on the chalkboard. She tells the girls that they will want to change their pads five or six times a day, then rushes through a description of tampons, which, because they haven't talked very specifically about That Hole, she does *not* demonstrate via the sketch.

Miss Jensen follows this up by pointing to a poster listing "do's" and "do-moderately's." There's no need to take a Menstrual Health Day, but she urges restraint. "You can bathe or shower, as long as you use warm water," she says. "And you can wash your hair, if you're sure to dry it quickly. And you can swim, if you wait until two or three days after the beginning of your period . . . And you can dance, but don't do any strenuous dancing like square dancing."

The final scene shows Molly in the living room with her family. Sister Jeanie comes down the stairs in a cloud of white tulle to meet a date. A voice-over tells us: "Soon, Molly will be a young woman like Jeanie. Having dates, going to dances in lovely, romantic dresses, and making new and important friends . . . Growing up. It's an exciting time." As the camera fades, Molly folds her hands beneath her chin, those same stars in her eyes, and dreamily aspires to her sister's more womanly state.

What's a young girl to make of all this? Well, thoroughly modern Molly tells us that girls ought to learn about bleeding from their moms; that the sexes ought to be segregated when they talk about it in school; that menstruation has something to do with reproduction, which has something to do with sex, which has something to do with boring old cells meetin' and greetin' in a fashion that's duller than church; that getting her period is synonymous with dating and romance (Belsky's mild-mannered ideological predecessor); that Mom is delighted to welcome her to womanhood (though Pop has his reservations), so she ought to be glad to be there—but however pleased Mom might be about "womanhood" in private, she doesn't mean a girl should ever let on about it publicly.

Mom Passes the Menstrual Modesty Torch

Let's begin with Mom, bearer of bad news. At the turn of the century, romantic engravings of mother-daughter duos, their heads inclined toward one another, their fingers laced, suggested a backdrop for "The Talk."[14] Mother was always the gentle, sympathetic messenger. In a 1915 instructional novel titled *Almost a Woman*, Mr. Wayne says suddenly to his wife, "I declare, Mary, our daughter Helen is almost a woman, isn't she?" When Mrs. Wayne agrees, the author propels us, with utter lack of subtlety or pretense, into "The Talk." "By the way," Mr. Wayne says, "You have always talked freely to her about life's mysteries; have you explained her approaching womanhood to her?" When Mrs. Wayne admits her negligence, Mr. Wayne chides her. "I beg of you not to postpone your instruction too long. I am more and more convinced that right knowledge not only safeguards purity, but really produces true modesty."[15]

And while the experts agree Mom is best suited for passing the menstrual modesty torch, they have consistently doubted her ability. In the early days, the authors of self-help books—usually doctors—were up-front about it. Bemoaning the masses of pitifully ignorant young girls out there, Dr. B. S. Talmey faulted moms quite overtly: "In the home, the mother, who has the child near her most of the time, is the chief offender," he wrote in *Genesis* (1910). Referring to an unenlightened relative who neglected to have "The Talk" with her daughter, he continued: "The answer was that she could not do it, and that whilst the necessity of an explanation was plain to her, she lacked the requisite knowledge to enlighten her child."[16] This mom—presumably of the eager and respectable middle class that most of these books were addressed to—was just uninformed. Other moms were hopelessly stupid. "In many cases parents cannot be taught how to impart information because they are of too low an order of intelligence to give instruction, even if they appreciate its value," Dr. Talmey went on to explain.[17]

That's why experts like himself felt compelled to step in. With the rise of this expert class in the early 1900s, doctors began to define menstruation for women. "All serious men and women agree that the masses need leading and guiding and constant suggestion," Dr. Talmey explained. Mothers, by virtue of their femaleness, were particularly susceptible to impaired reasoning. Thus the experts began to create specific material to orchestrate these mother-daughter chats. "My aim has been to reach the average woman, and simplicity and understandability have been my objectives throughout," Dr. Emil Novak wrote in his 1937 instructional book called *The Woman Asks the Doctor.* Consequently the text was dumbed down for the ladies. "Not a 'statistic' is given," he promised, "and there are no references and practically no citations from original sources, for these would interfere with easy readability and continuity."[18]

By the 1950s, as the sanitary protection industry took over the job of educating and advising mothers about educating and advising offspring, it offered neighborly tips. (The medical legacy endured, but Miss Jensen–style: I'm not a doctor, but I play one on TV.) Wisely, the industry insinuated itself into the advisory role. *How Shall I Tell My Daughter?*, the makers of Modess titled their 1970 pamphlet on menstruation. Asking "Can we help?" Modess offered a "Mother-Daughter Starter Kit," which contained "everything a mother needs to discuss menstruation with her young daughter"—plus, of course, some sample products.

While the 1981 Tampax survey of Americans' attitudes toward menstruation indicates that the majority of women, 64 percent, first learned about menstruation from their mothers, the makers of menstrual products have long worried about what Mom was saying. Could she be trusted to impart the right information? They didn't think so. The new material didn't exactly undermine Mom, it simply began—in the mid-1970s—to leave her out of the picture altogether. The sanitary protection industry positioned itself as the new authority.

When Molly grew up in the 1950s, the industry still paid tribute to Mom's role. For good reason. Mom is Molly's first source and confidante, making it clear that menstruation is a private, girl-talk, family matter. Nice girls may talk about bleeding in the privacy of their fluffy, girlish bedrooms, but nice girls never talk about it elsewhere. The fact that so much of this material was actually created for and presented in the schools made the idea of intimate mother-daughter scenarios somewhat disingenuous. But the message was specific: the schools—or the industry—may have taken over educating girls about this, but it's still properly a personal matter (thus Personal Products, etc.), best dealt with in the home. So while menstrual education may have come out of the closet, it was only to revere the good old days when it had properly remained there.

By the 1990s, the scenario had flipped. While in the 1950s Molly's mother was seen as the primary source of information, with the school nurse filling in the gaps, today the industry posits itself as the primary source, with parents playing a supporting role. Tambrands' current teaching guide suggests that educators send girls home with instructional pamphlets. "These take-home materials might help clear up misunderstandings and educate parents, as well as the children, in a non-threatening way," the company writes.[19]

The Sex-Segregated Classroom

In the 1980s the omniscient expert took the form of the voice-over. Consider Tambrands' current teaching kit, which includes a video titled *Kids to Kids*. The movie, in a desperate attempt at hipness, features MTV-style fast cuts, boppy music, and cinema-verité pubescents rappin' about zits, boobs, and periods. Two groups of Connecticut middle-school kids—separated by gender—speculate about their bodily changes on camera. Each segment is punctuated by a benign adult voice-over that corrects misinformation and gives teens more appropriate words and explanations for menstruation.

The information presented is accurate and generally helpful. Yes, menstruation is a normal part of growing up, the industry-generated material tells girls in "The Movie" they're yanked from gym class to see — once. But for the rest of their lives girls face a barrage of ads that contradict this, ads that fuel paranoia about bleeding while boosting product sales.

Sometimes educational material is used to lay the groundwork for ads. To ensure a continued emphasis on the private, personal nature of bleeding, the companies emphasize the new guardians of decorum: boys. Today, advertising directed at teens emphasizes just how embarrassing it would be for boys to learn that a girl's bleeding. And to set the stage for that anxiety, Tambrands reminds educators of the importance of sex-segregated classes: "If the program is to be taught to a mixed group, we strongly recommend that additional time be allowed for teaching about menstruation in more detail with the girls alone." In suggesting that girls may be more comfortable discussing this in sex-segregated groups, the company reinforces the notion that such a setting is the only appropriate venue.

Would girls be more comfortable asking questions in an all-girl class? If so, why is that? What messages have they already internalized about periods, and will pulling boys from the classroom counter or reinforce that? Good puberty educators, like skilled sex-ed teachers, have devised a simple solution to the "embarrassing question" dilemma: students anonymously write their questions on slips of paper and the teacher systematically reads and answers them.

But Tambrands eschews this method. While it has agreed to call its curriculum "puberty education" and to talk about changes in boys as well as girls, it clings to the sex-segregated forum. This is partly a concession to convention, but also a convenient way to keep menstruation private and embarrassing.

Ads, like this one that Tambrands ran in various teen magazines in the 1990s, nurture the seeds of worry planted in the educational material:

> You may do a lot of things to get noticed, wearing a pad shouldn't be one of them. If you're wearing a pad you may just be announcing to everyone that you have your period. No matter how thin or "discreet" they say they've made pads, can they stand up to a pair of leggings? Tampax tampons can because they're worn on the inside where they can protect you sooner and no one can tell you're using them.

The two girls pictured in the ad may be dressing up and acting goofy to get the guys' attention, but, the copy tells us, if boys are privy to their periods, the girls can kiss romance good-bye.

Both reflecting and reinforcing cultural squeamishness, the feminine hygiene industry slyly protects its profits. Worried girls double up tampons and pads, wear protection on the days they *might* get their periods, and fret enough to don the daily protection advertisers now remind them should be "worn between periods to absorb normal vaginal discharge."[20] How effective is the tactic? One 1997 British survey discovered that as many as one in five young women use panty liners *between* periods as part of everyday hygiene.[21]

Skirting S-E-X: The Language of Bleeding

Menstrual education has never been subject to the same kind of scrutiny and censure as sex education, but it suffers by association. With both, parents divide themselves into two camps:

those who think information about sex and reproduction is the purview of parents, and those who think schools should play a role in educating kids about sex. The only thing the two sides agree on is that the wrong source for kids to get the facts of life from is their peers. For hundreds of years, experts have been reminding parents of the dangers of information gleaned "on the streets." The contemporary reasons given for promoting organized menstrual ed in particular, and sex ed in general, are that peers are unreliable, a source of misinformation.

This is obviously true. But a hidden agenda sets the stage for both sex and menstrual education. "Forbidding to speak about sexual matters causes rather the mind to occupy itself with this subject and awakens the morbid curiosity regarding the mysteries of sex," Talmey wrote in his *Genesis*.[22] He condemned any "fig-leaf policy" that might draw a child's attention to the fact that there was something to be concealed. "When they are not prepared, boys become greatly excited at the first seminal emission, and girls still more at the first appearance of menstruation."[23] Talmey attributed the authority of "scientific proof" to this observation, insisting, "It is a physiological fact that accurate knowledge on these points excites the least those pupils who were instructed in these matters before their sexual awakening."[24] Sex education was a way of curbing desire.

With girls, there was a limit to how long parents could put off "The Talk": menarche. Experts urged parents to act quickly, lest lust get hold of their children before they did. "Another watch-care at this time is due, because . . . sometimes the sex-instinct is more active, also self-control is diminished following the period," William Forbush wrote in his 1919 volume *The Sex Education of Children*.[25]

The connection between menstruation and sex has long worried parents. If their children began speculating about anything down there, including menstruation, it would be only a matter of time until the conversation devolved into raunchy talk about sex. In no way should periods be titillating. And the language of menstrual ed is testament to that.

In earlier days this language was often so convoluted that it was nearly incomprehensible. Strange metaphors littered the pages of sex-ed tracts. There are the birds and the bees, of course. (And the beauty of this scenario, which I never fully appreciated until my recent forays into this material, is that with bees, fertilization of flowers takes place without intercourse. Or even touching.) A 1919 book, in deference to the ovum-as-egg image, refers to a girl's reproductive organs as "the three little nests." My favorite passage, though, requires a return to Dr. Mary Wood-Allen's 1915 *Almost a Woman*, in which Mrs. Wayne chooses to describe the event architecturally to her daughter, Helen:

> "Why, mother, don't we just grow into women?"
>
> "Well, my dear, I shall have to say both yes and no to that question. Girls do grow and become women, but women are something more than grown-up girls. This house is much bigger than it was two years ago. Did it just grow bigger?"
>
> "Why, no, not exactly. There are no more rooms now than there were before, but some rooms have been finished off and are used now, when before they weren't used at all, and so the house seems bigger. But it can't be

that way with our bodies, for we don't have any new organs added or finished off to make us women?"

"That is just what is done, my daughter."

"What! New organs added, mother? What can you mean?"

"I mean, dear, that your bodily dwelling is enlarged, not by the addition of new rooms, but by the completing of rooms that have as yet not been fitted up for use . . ."[26]

Even when the language is more straightforward, it is always dry and clinical. The just-the-facts sketches—and even today, they are always illustrations and never photos—of vaginas, labia, uteruses, and ovaries say, "This is all about sex, but look how dull and un-fun it is." "From fission to parturition, reproduction is self-sacrifice," a 1910 text explains. It's always a downer. The womb is weeping. Menstruation is "an expression of disappointment on the part of the endometrium at the failure of pregnancy to occur," according to Emil Novak's 1937 book *The Woman Asks the Doctor*.[27] Talmey's *Genesis*, published in 1910, describes it in economic terms, as "the getting rid of some material whose function has been frustrated and for which the economy has no use any more."[28]

Even today, menstruation is a sad story, depicted in the literature as "disintegration," "decay," "shrinking," "shedding," "discharge," "dribbling," and "sloughing." Feminist Emily Martin described the language of menstruation in her 1987 book *The Woman in the Body* as revolving around "the central metaphor of failed production of a baby."[29] Contrasting it to the language of ejaculation, in which boys "manufacture," "harden," "flood," "swim," "race," and "spurt," it's easy to see why girls might think, obvious inconveniences aside, that bleeding is one big bummer. "Menstruation not only carries with it the connotation of a production system that has failed to produce, it also carries the idea of production gone awry, making products of no use, not to specification, unsalable, wasted, scrap," Martin writes. "However disgusting it may be, menstrual blood will come out. Production gone awry is also an image that fills us with dismay and horror."[30]

But writing solely about failed production poses a bit of a problem for educators. If menstruation is what happens when an egg *isn't* fertilized, kids are sure to wonder what happens when an egg *is* fertilized. The peculiar language of the "feminine hygiene" curriculums reflects the quandary adults find themselves in. It is very hard to explain menstruation without explaining sex.

But that is exactly what happens. Consistently. "In deference to prevailing prejudices on this subject, a scientific discussion of the anatomy and physiology of the external sex organs of the human body and of copulation have been entirely omitted," Talmey wrote in *Genesis*.[31] Although there have been exceptions—notably in the writings of sex-ed crusader Mary Ware Dennett and in pamphlets put out by the sanitary protection industry for a brief period during the freewheeling 1960s and early 1970s—the idea that sex should be avoided persists today. For sanitary protection companies trying to reach the broadest group of consumers without alienating anyone, tiptoeing around S-E-X was vital to their continued success. Personal Products Corporation told educators in 1978 that they should reassure parents that they were talking about periods. Period. "In particular, it may be important to differentiate feminine development programs from sex education," the company suggested.

Typically, the closest industry gets to sex is this 1995 passage from a Tambrands pamphlet, *A Time for Answers:*

> Once a boy goes through puberty, his body begins producing sperm. Sperm are male reproductive cells. Pregnancy begins when an egg and a sperm cell join together. This joining together is called fertilization.[32]

No one in industry-manufactured educational material ever copulates, has sex, engages in intercourse, or even makes love. (Boys *do* get the occasional inconvenient erection or nocturnal emission, but the biological impetus behind such unruly genitals is not discussed.) If kids are curious about the mysterious presence of semen in the uterus, they'll remain that way—at least according to most official curriculums—until they take sex ed in the tenth or eleventh grade. Indeed, Tambrands' 1997 description of the vagina describes a host of visitors, but omits the penis. "Most of the time, the walls of the vagina lie flat against each other," the 1997 pamphlet explains. "But they can expand a lot to allow a baby to pass through, or a little to hold a tampon."[33] (How *did* that baby get there?)

Menstrual Myths

Back at camp, I took a break from interviewing girls to attend an evening campfire meeting, for counselors only. Chitchatting with staff and regaling them with tales of the misinformation that's out there—one girl worried that inserting a tampon was the equivalent of "doing the nasty"; another said she'd never use plugs because she might get "electric shock syndrome"—I mentioned that concerns about bathing and swimming were still, even in 1997, oddly prevalent. Although I originally attributed the swimming thing to logistical difficulties—if you've exclusively used pads, like many new menstruaters, that could be a significant barrier to water play—that turned out not to be the reason. In fact, many girls thought it was bad for you, physically, to swim, shower, or bathe while bleeding. (Indeed, the Tampax survey showed that even as late as 1981, 22 percent of Americans still believed swimming and bathing during menstruation were harmful.[34])

One counselor at the campfire, who came from the Deep South, said her grandmother had always told her that same thing. "She said you were more prone to catching diseases then because your pores are more open."

Two other counselors, college-educated, in their late twenties, chimed in. "It's funny how some of these old wives' tales turn out to be true," one of them mused. Her friend agreed. "Yeah, that actually does make sense that, since your pores are more open then, it's probably easier for germs to enter."

"I read somewhere that now they're discovering there's something to these things, like old herbal remedies that they realize today actually work," her friend added.

As the counselors drifted away on an echinacea tangent, I sat there silent, fascinated by how readily the women had embraced the water myth as fact. Why did they think menstruation made your pores open up? Why, against all logic, would they think bathing or swimming more likely to propel these germs into the allegedly larger pores?

The next day, as I continued my interviews and listened to the campers struggling to explain just what menstruation was, I realized that educators typically rely on a solitary lesson to explain menstruation. Unlike instruction in, say, plant growth, in which lessons on photosynthesis are first taught in a simplistic form in the primary grades and then are repeated and elaborated on every couple of years thereafter, menstrual education, like so many sex-ed programs, is a one-shot deal. And menstrual instruction, unlike sex ed, often relies entirely on a curriculum created and peddled by sanitary protection companies. The industry's point of view is the only one young girls hear in the schools. And the industry struggles valiantly to debunk one set of unprofitable myths while promoting another set with more lucrative potential.

The myths (what some old fogies think you should do while bleeding) and the rules (what *we* think you should do while bleeding) form the bulk of the lesson plan today. Since studies show that 38 percent of Americans think virgins shouldn't use tampons, that myth is public enemy number one.[35] In each and every booklet, pamphlet, instructional video, or Q&A blurb, Tambrands assures girls that "a virgin is someone who has not had sexual intercourse." Not to worry. "Using a tampon has nothing to do with losing your virginity."[36]

They also assure girls that tampons can't get "lost" inside them, that menstruating women can wash their hair to no ill effect, that cold drinks don't cause menstrual cramps, etc.[37] They tell students that menstruation is normal and healthy and happens to all women, and then, with a subtle bait-and-switch, assure them that no one need know about theirs. To a hypothetical question—"Can anyone tell if I have my period?"—Tambrands answers no: "Unless you tell someone, it's your secret." And, by the way, in order to keep it that way, here's some advice. Use tampons, not pads, "so you don't have to worry about odor."[38] Use biodegradable tampons and applicators, since flushing them down the toilet is "a good way to help keep your period private."[39] Don't go touching or exploring around there; use applicators, which are more hygienic, "since the fingers do not touch the tampon or the vagina."[40]

As they sketch out the rules, today's sanitary protection companies rely on groundwork laid down by their predecessors. Portraying menstruation as a time when girls need to redouble their efforts to "be [their] most attractive self" is easy, because the experts have been warning girls about the very troublesome nature of bleeding for years. In *The Married Woman's Private Medical Companion* (1854), Dr. A. M. Mauriceau reminded girls:

> The stomach and bowels, at this period, are very easily disordered, and therefore, everything which is heavy or indigestible, ought to be avoided. Some are hurt by eating fruits or vegetables; others by taking fermented liquor . . . Exposure to cold, particularly getting the feet wet, is hurtful, as it tends suddenly to obstruct the discharge. The same effect is likewise produced by violent passions of the mind, which are also, at this time, peculiarly apt to excite spasmodic affections, or hysterical fits.[41]

By 1995, things have changed—somewhat. In a book called *Everything You Need to Know About Getting Your Period*—

which, incidentally, is part of "The Need to Know Library" series of grimly titled books like *An Alcoholic Parent, AIDS, Date Rape, Incest, Street Gangs, Teen Suicide*, etc.—author Nancy Rue responds to the question "How will I know when my period will start?" with this optimistic list of symptoms:

> Some girls notice their stomachs looking and feeling bloated. Others have warning cramps, or their back hurts or their breasts are tender. The following are the most common symptoms: queasy stomach or cramps; swollen, tender breasts; a major outbreak of pimples; emotional feelings; hair oilier than usual; more perspiration than usual; a little weight gain; tense and irritable feelings; unusual hunger and thirst; fatigue or an "I don't care" attitude; lower back ache; and headache.[42]

Obviously, some of these signs may be present when a girl menstruates, but to the uninitiated, in aggregate, they're terrifying. To forestall such trauma, Dr. A. M. Mauriceau suggested in his 1854 book that menstruating women curb their activities, warning that "dancing, exposure to much heat, or making any great or fatiguing exertion, are improper."[43] By 1981, Kimberly-Clark is encouraging girls to exercise, since it's "one way to build a firm figure," but continues to warn young women, "Don't overdo during your periods."[44] A 1990 book by Eric Johnson called *Love and Sex and Growing Up* echoes this ancient wisdom, suggesting that "during the early part of her menstrual period, a girl may want to cut down on strenuous games and play."[45]

Tambrands, on the other hand, has always countered this rule by highlighting athletic women in its ads. It urges girls to exercise while menstruating but adds a caveat: redouble your efforts then to prevent leakage. In the late 1980s Tambrands produced a "Dance Away: Get Fit with the Hits" aerobic video series for teens, which it promoted with this plug: "And remember, with Petal Soft Tampax you can still exercise during your period, comfortably and without the embarrassment of accidents or bulky pads." To keep the stakes high, the company implies that "your little secret" is safe, but precarious, with it. Worry, they tell girls, because evidence of your bleeding is an omnipresent threat.

For a hundred and fifty years, from the earliest health tracts to the most recent pamphlets, educators have professed a single mission: to allay girls' fears about menstruation so that they come to view it as a natural part of womanhood. A worthwhile endeavor. But in the battle for the bodies and minds of adolescent girls, the subtext screams louder than words.

UNOFFICIAL CURRICULUMS: THE SUBTEXT

"My mom doesn't talk to me about that stuff," Rosie says to the other girls gathered on the grass at camp.

Rebecca takes pleasure in being allowed to talk about it. "We're talking about periods," she shouts to a counselor walking across the lawn. "It's very bloody!"

Laura, too, welcomes the chance to ask questions. "Have you ever wondered how you use those long thingys?" she says.

"Tampons," Missy says. "My mom says they go between your privates."

"Ohhh."

"My mom told me what the private is," Rebecca says. The group grows silent, expectant. But Rebecca simply points. "Down there," she says. Another counselor passes by and she announces again, at the top of her lungs, "We're talking about periods!" She turns to me. "Do you think we're being gross?"

I tell her no.

"Really?" she says.

I shrug.

"You know what my mom told me once?" Missy asks. "She said boys' minds are in their privates and that's why they're so disgusting."

Another counselor goes by. "Miss Lilly!" Rebecca shouts. "We're talking about periods." Rebecca thinks for a minute, then yells out a follow-up. "Have you had your period?" The counselor tells her yes. Rebecca turns to me. "I hope I'm not being rude," she says, "But do you think all the staff here has had their periods?"

I tell her I expect so.

Laura wants to return to the topic of sanitary protection. "My mom keeps those *things* . . ."

"Pads," Missy corrects again.

". . . in the cupboard in the bathroom. When I saw them, I said, 'What are these for?'"

"Once when my mother was changing her clothes, I saw . . . her *thing* in her pants," Sandra says softly. "I didn't say anything, though."

"You saw it?" Rebecca asks, impressed.

"Are you gay?" Rosie asks.

"It's not gay, if you see a girl," Missy says. "My mom walks around the house naked."

"But if you see a girl's *thing*?" Rosie says.

"Pad," Missy corrects.

"Period!" Rebecca says. "Period! Period!" She turns to me. "Do you think we're being naughty?"

———————

The messages girls internalize about periods start early. Whatever and however girls learn about periods today, by the time they have them as adolescents, they're embarrassed. Nowhere is this clearer than in the teen magazines they devour like junk food.

In 1994, *Seventeen* magazine debuted a new column. Editors called it "Trauma-rama," asking teens to write in about "their most embarrassing moments." "Share your shame," the magazine urged its readers, setting seasonally appropriate themes: a back-to-school "Halls of Shame" warned girls that "crowded classrooms, halls and even bathrooms give you a large, gossipy audience for all your goofiest mistakes"; a Christmas "Shop of Horrors" cautioned teens that "when you shop till you drop, you can fall into some serious embarrassments"; and a less time-specific "Boy Trouble" column warned that "it's extremely embarrassing when girl-meets-boy meets disaster." According to *Seventeen* Senior Features Editor Robert Rorke, "Trauma-rama," which runs on the first content page of every issue, is extremely popular among its 2.5 million readers. "It's our most read column," he says. Like *Teen* magazine, which runs a similarly hot column called "Why Me? Your Horror Stories and Ultimate Embarrassments" on its last content page, and *YM*'s comparable "Say Anything: Your Most Humiliating Experiences," menstrual mortification is a constant theme.

"*Most* of what I get in the mail is about menstruation," says "Trauma-rama" editor Melanie Mannarino. "Practically every other letter has to do with getting your period. I could sign on to my e-mail tomorrow and I'm sure I'll have a bunch of letters about menstruation and some embarrassing moment." For the most part, Mannarino tosses the letters because her personal policy is to limit "period" stories to one a month. She's sure she'll get more the next day. "And believe it or not, all these letters we run are real," she says.

The stories are revealing. One, titled "Maxi Mortification," in *Seventeen*'s November 1996 issue, reads this way:

> I was getting ready for a date when my period arrived unexpectedly. In a rush, I yelled downstairs to my mother, "I need some pads, I'm leaking everywhere—it's so disgusting!" Little did I know, my date was waiting at the end of the stairs. He hardly touched me all night.

The *YM*, *Teen*, and *Seventeen* letters are full of such stories, tales in which girls are unwittingly outed, their periods made public, a fact they lament with an I-bleed-therefore-I'm-yucky tagline. In a single, expanded "Why Me?" section in the November 1994 *Teen*, seven out of thirty letters were about periods. These "grossest, most horrifying, mortifying moments" have to do with (1) bleeding through a white dress while meeting your boyfriend's parents for the first time; (2) falling asleep at a slumber party and having your friends stick tampons up your nose, then answering the door with strings hanging out of your nose the next morning . . . and it's your boyfriend!; (3) falling down while roller-skating in a short skirt and being sure your "pad was showing and everything"; (4) being at the drug-store and striking up a conversation with "a really hot guy," then having your little sister convey a message from Mom, a few aisles over, about whether to buy deodorant or nondeodor-ant tampons; (5) accidentally running into the boys' bathroom at school and shouting out for a *boy* to get you a tampon from the dispenser; (6) sitting on a guy's lap and having your period go through your shorts and onto his shorts; (7) being at cheer-leading tryouts, having your pad fall out, and having your chums tease you forever after for being "a bloody Barbie Doll."

Many of the "Trauma-rama" and "Why Me?" letters are leakage stories, which makes sense. Of course it's a drag when you ruin a pair of shorts, bleed onto the living-room couch, stain a pair of panties. What is curious, though, is the number of "I nearly died" stories that have to do with simply acknowl-edging that you menstruate. Or that you *may* menstruate. Or that you *may have* menstruated in the past. Tampons that fall out of book bags, boys who see you purchasing pads, o.b.s that slip out of pockets—all the accoutrements that make your pri-vate shame public are cause for alarm.

Not surprisingly, those studying this phenomenon find it pervasive. Lenore Williams, a nurse-educator who conducted a study of nine-to-twelve-year-old girls in 1983, discovered that 30 percent thought menstruation was embarrassing, 27 per-cent thought it was disgusting, and 23 percent worried about the fact that it was "uncontrollable." Eighty-five percent thought that girls should not talk to boys about their periods.

Though the study is more than a decade old, it's obvious, from the letters in these teen magazines, that the attitude persists.[46]

In one fairly typical letter from the March 1995 *Teen* "Why Me?" column, a girl writes,

> I was at school, when I noticed that I had started my period early. Since I didn't have a pad, my teacher gave me an office pass to get one. When I got to the office, I saw two of the finest guys in school sitting against the wall. I didn't want them to know why I was there, so I whispered my problem in the secretary's ear. To my horror, she turned around and said in a loud voice, "Hey Nancy, could you get this girl a pad please!" She then handed the pad to me right in front of the two guys, and they started to laugh. I could have died!

This letter writer worries that if boys know she bleeds, they won't like her. It's not about the inconveniences of menstruation, it's about the stigma.

With this anecdote, like all of them, I found I had to read it twice. The first time, I read it and thought, "Yeah, that would be embarrassing." The second time, I read it and thought, "Why would this be embarrassing?" Is it because blood is dirty? Is it because it comes from "down there" and "down there" is where sex happens? Is it because your period reminds boys that you touch yourself "down there". . . even if it is only to press a pad into place or push a tampon in?

Maybe. But this seepage also signals a loss of control over the body. It's embarrassing for this girl because her body has betrayed her. Nice girls don't bleed. (Well, of course they do!)

Okay then, nice girls don't let on that they bleed. Nice girls control their bodies.

After all, these menstrual moments are nestled among dozens of other "leaky body" stories. Teenage girls, whose bodies have begun to betray them, write about "goo" spilling out of all their orifices. From sweat patches on a prom dress, to vomiting in public, to laughing so hard that soda, snot, or nachos squirt out of their noses. One girl sneezes and farts at the same time . . . in church. Another climbs on a guy's shoulders to hang Christmas ornaments, then laughs so hard she farts. A third slow-dances with the boy of her dreams, giggles when her best friend makes faces from the sidelines, then laughs so hard she farts. (To which her date responds, "Wow! I felt the vibes from that one!")[47] My favorite fart yarn ran in the December 1994 *Teen*. A girl's mother blindfolds her to present her birthday surprise. The girl writes:

> [Mom] brought me to the dining room table and sat me down. The phone rang and she told me not to peek while she answered it. She left the room. Since I had beans at my friend's house earlier, I farted really really loud. I made sure my mom was still on the phone, then I farted again! This time it smelled like rotten eggs! I did this for about five minutes. My mom finally came back and she uncovered my blindfold, and I saw my surprise! Twelve of my best friends and my boyfriend sitting around our table as a birthday surprise! I was mortified! . . .

Farts, of course, always elicit laughs. But somewhere along the way, prepubescent hysteria and girlish giggles turn into "mortification." Your body and its effluents, once the subject of hilarity, become the stuff of nightmares.

This thing, which was once just simply *you*, has now taken on a life of its own. Your breasts and hips are growing. You leak: your vagina drips, you sweat, you bleed. And everything you read and see on TV tells you to hide these facts. Even the accoutrements you need to attend to these changes are cause for embarrassment. They blow your cover. In the October 1995 *Teen*, "L.G." from Indiana writes:

> I was at softball practice. I had changed right before and stuffed all my clothes, including my bra, in my backpack. My friend and a couple of guys we like were hanging out, watching me practice. My friend asked to borrow my brush and I told her it was in my backpack. When she went to get it, she pulled everything out, including my bra! . . .

And it's not just undergarments that are embarrassing. One girl, who "wore a strapless black dress to [the] Christmas dance" wrote to *Teen*, "I wanted to die when I got to the dance and my best friend told me that you could see deodorant under my arms!" Another girl was horrified when her dog trotted into the room with a tampon applicator in its mouth. "It wouldn't have been so bad if my boyfriend hadn't been joining us for dinner!" she laments.[48]

Tampon and pad ads—which in *Teen* magazine are often conveniently slotted to appear on the page opposite "Why Me?"—reinforce this. "No one ever has to know: 1. You still use a night-light. 2. You sing show tunes in the shower. 3. Your parents were hippies," Stayfree promises *Teen* readers in ads that run month after month. "And no one ever has to know you have your period." (Advertisers drop the point size down several notches on the word *period*, for emphasis: Shhhhh.)[49] A 1994 Kotex ad in the magazine runs this copy next to a drawing labeled "Your Boyfriend's Sweater:" "Hey, when your clothes move around, it's comfortable. When your maxi does, it's gross." (Here, the point-size swells, while the font puffs up and bloats on the last word.) A series of 1994 Tampax ads that run in *Teen* and *Seventeen* borrows a format from the popular advice columns that proliferate in these magazines by having hypothetical teens write in to two "experts" for tampon tips. The "experts" are "Marcia, R.N." (who lends legitimacy with her medical credentials) and "Anne, 19 yrs" (who lends legitimacy with her near-peer colloquialisms). When "Charlene, age 13" writes in, complaining that girls at her school have to carry plastic applicators out of their stalls to the bathroom's sole trash basket, "Anne" commiserates with her. "Taking a pad or plastic applicator to the trash is like wearing a sign that says 'I have my period!'" she laments, reminding Charlene that Tampax Flushable Applicator Tampons are "neater, easier and *much less embarrassing*."[50]

In some ways, this ad is pushing the concealment element even further than most women go in their everyday lives. After all, while women tend to hide menstruation from men, letting on to other women that you're bleeding is usually fine. In fact, asking to borrow a tampon or some ibuprofen can almost be an overture of friendship, entrusting a colleague or acquaintance with your secrets.

Indeed, author Emily Martin speculates in *The Woman in the Body* that shared confidences in the bathroom occasionally have a subversive effect, this being one of the areas in which women have traditionally gathered to commune with one another and kvetch—though now that more bosses are women, a quick peep beneath the stall doors has been added to the routine. Describing the bathroom as a "complex backstage area in contrast to the school, factory, or firm's public front stage area," Martin notes that documents dating back to the turn of the century contain references to girls in the washroom "fussing over the universe," sobbing over "stolen wages," and "reading union leaflets posted in the washroom during a difficult struggle to organize a clothing factory."[51] "The double-edged nature of the shame of women's bodily functions here works in their favor: if private places must be provided to take care of what is shameful and disgusting, then those private places can be used in subversive ways," Martin says. For young girls today, that tradition is alive and well. They smoke in the girls' room, they hide out there when skipping class, they copy homework there. It's also a haven they use to define themselves by putting on makeup and talking about boys, sex, and teachers they hate. It's one of the few places where girls and women can relax their artifices for a while. But the Tampax ad pushes the parameters of taboo, suggesting that girls need to hide their menstrual paraphernalia, even in this time-honored "free space."

Part of what makes these fear-of-exposure ads effective is that they play to the subconscious belief on the part of many girls—and women—that they actually look different when they're menstruating. (Remember that the 1981 Tampax report found that 27 percent of Americans believed that women looked different when they were menstruating—and an amazing 49 percent believed they smelled different.)

The sanitary protection industry, of course, capitalizes on these beliefs. Though the 1981 Tampax report is the only one the company ever allowed the public—mostly academics—to get their hands on, we can assume that contemporary marketing surveys are telling them this fear is alive and well. Why else run ads like the one in the September 1997 issue of *Seventeen*? "You know the feeling. It's when you're absolutely positive that everybody in the universe knows you're having your period. You feel different, you feel like you look different . . . and those pads aren't exactly what you'd call discreet. Ugh."

And articles in the magazines also do their part to promote that view. For example, a 1995 *Mademoiselle* article titled "Beauty and the Beast: How Your Period Affects Your Looks" reminds its teenage and twenty-something readers that "you can't look good when you feel like pond scum." Describing "erupting skin" and "raccoon eyes" as a "monthly beauty slump," the magazine concedes that there's "absolutely nothing a woman can't do when she has her period, but, *entre nous*, there are a few things you might want to keep in mind for the sake of your looks . . ." The difference between "looking good and looking like you're on the rag" is nutrition, exercise, stress reduction, and, of course, a few brand-name creams and cleansers like "Aroma Vera Feminine Energy," "Bare Escentuals," and, for "the offshore rig on your face," "Cetaphil Gentle Cleaning Bar" or "Exact Vanishing Cream." And it's not just your looks; your judgment suffers. Don't make any major decisions, like getting your hair cut because "it may sound brilliant now, but you could regret it later." Follow these steps, though, and "your looks don't have to run amok along with your hormones." And remember, tackling those "dark circles, broken capillaries, puffy eyes" shows character and fortitude. After all, "these are the days that separate the women from the girls."[52]

The "girls," for their part, pick up on the cues. Like Margaret in Judy Blume's *Are You There God?*, they may be excited about getting their period before it happens, but when the reality sets in, with the one-two punch of genuine inconvenience and manufactured embarrassment, they view things differently. A 1988 study by Wellesley College Center for Research on Women discovered a pronounced difference between girls anticipating their periods and those having recently gotten them. The former were excited, the latter were "grossed out."

A group of thirteen-, fourteen-, and fifteen-year-olds whom I interviewed at the camp in the Catskills certainly described their periods in negative terms. They believed they were different when they were menstruating. "You're butt-ugly," fourteen-year-old Tanya explained. But worse than that—or perhaps as a result of that belief—her confidence suffers. "When people say stuff to me, when people are complimenting you, you don't believe them. You doubt everybody then," she said. Her thirteen-year-old friend, Mary, put it more succinctly: "You feel more self-conscious." Tanya agreed. And worried. "Some guys say they can tell [you're having your period]," she said. "But I hope not."

Every bodily function has the potential to betray girls. In the

November 1995 "Why Me?" column, "P.C." from Hawaii writes:

> One day I went to the movies with my dad and I really had to use the bathroom. While we were walking out of the movie theater, I told my dad I needed to stop at the rest room. I noticed a couple of guys from school waiting near the rest rooms, so I decided not to go in. My dad stopped and said, "I thought you had to use the bathroom!" Even after I told him I didn't, he said, really loud, "But you told me you had to go!" When the guys heard us, they started laughing.

The sheer fact that she has to acknowledge bodily needs, that these boys now realize she pees, devastates her. Puberty—this extended process in which girls' bodies change in ways they cannot control—can cause absolute panic. It's a phenomenon Simone de Beauvoir remarked on nearly fifty years ago in *The Second Sex*:

> The young girl feels that her body is getting away from her, it is no longer the straightforward expression of her individuality; it becomes foreign to her; and at the same time she becomes for others a thing: on the street men follow her with their eyes and comment on her anatomy. She would like to be invisible; it frightens her to become flesh and to show her flesh.

De Beauvoir points to menarche as the moment when bodily realities intrude on any Peter Pan perpetual-child fantasies a girl might have. This hygienic crisis appears like a slap in the face (perhaps explaining the origins of a still-common Jewish ritual: slapping a girl when she gets her first period), an irrefutable sign that girls must move from the relative freedom of childhood into the more restrictive gender roles of womanhood. "Previously the little girl, with a bit of self-deception, could consider herself as still a sexless being," de Beauvoir writes. "Or she could think of herself not at all; she might even dream of awakening changed into a man; but now, mothers and aunties whisper flatteringly: 'She's a big girl now' and the matrons' group has won: she belongs to it." Puberty and menarche are embarrassing for girls, de Beauvoir speculates, because their bodies, unpredictable and out of control, are taking them some place they're loath to go: womanhood. "She is neither gold nor diamond," de Beauvoir writes, "but a strange form of matter, ever-changing, indefinite, deep within which unclean alchemies are in the course of elaboration."[53]

Fueling this anxiety is a culture that feels free to comment on and pick apart a girl's body. Suddenly, people are looking at her body and talking about her body. "She scents danger in her alienated flesh," de Beauvoir writes.

Flash-forward four decades and Paula Vogel is writing about this same phenomenon in her semi-autobiographical 1997 play *How I Learned to Drive.* In a scene that takes place around the supper table, a teenager's breasts become fair game for commentary. The girl, Li'l Bit, is scrutinized and talked about as if she isn't even present. "Look, Grandma. Li'l Bit's getting to be as big in the bust as you are," the mother says. Soon the grandfather chimes in. "Yup," he says. "If Li'l Bit gets any bigger, we're gonna haveta buy her a wheelbarrow to carry in front of her." Later, he suggests, "We could write to Kate Smith. Ask her for somma her used brassieres she don't want anymore—she could maybe give to Li'l Bit here . . ." Li'l Bit, understandably, complains about the direction the conversation's taken. "I tell you, Grandma, Li'l Bit's at that age," says the mother. "She's so sensitive, you can't say boo." Her grandfather goes on: "Well, she'd better stop being so sensitive. 'Cause five minutes before Li'l Bit turns the corner, her tits turn first . . ."[54]

This is a fictional account of growing up in an admittedly bizarre family, but it serves as an overt example of this phenomenon. As girls enter puberty, folks begin to comment on their bodies. They are supposed to both ignore and elicit this reaction. This is not news. Feminists have been putting forward this complaint for several decades: girls (and women) are encouraged to look sexy, but not to act on it; to be the object but not the subject of desire. In an effort to perpetuate this belief, the teen magazines push girls to view themselves as two separate entities, body and self—a contemporary variation of the oppositional patterns of Western thinking, which has traditionally pitted body against soul. The magazines remind girls that there is their baser body—including its fat, pimples, sexual desire, and menstrual effluent—which they must control, and then there is their true self. The teen magazines—and the women's magazines these readers will graduate to—are full of advice on how to "dress up your looks," "brush up on your best beauty bets," and "get a thinner, foxier, cuter body this summer," while simultaneously counseling girls who write to the advice columns to date boys who like them for who they are, not for what they look like.

What's Sex Got to Do With It?
Making Sense of the Sex-Blood Link

In today's teen magazines, nurturing of the self takes the form of Feminism Lite. An article in the August 1994 *Teen* borrows directly from the cultural feminists, women who think it's woman's nature to nurture and who look forward to a kinder, gentler world run by women, who are . . . well, just nicer than men. In "Why It's Great to Be a Girl," the editors remind readers, "You're a real '90s girl—smart, stylish, determined to make the most of yourself and your life. Sure, guys have a lot of great qualities. But, hey, let's face it—girls excel! For added evidence of the intelligence, sensitivity and overall coolness of the female species, check out some of these facts." Readers learn that women invented disposable diapers, bras, and drip coffee makers; that they see better in the dark, smell better than men, and make decisions faster. (Oddly enough, in a section about power, the editors chirp that things have "changed since our mom's day, when the boy was the student council president, and the girl was the secretary!"—and then cite Hillary Clinton, *wife* of a man in power, as an example.) However misguided this cultural feminist approach may be, it is at least an effort to encourage girls to cultivate their intellect. Sort of.

But the Fem Lite articles are as antithetical to the beauty tips as the ads are to the editorial content. (For example, *Seventeen* suggests that menstrual candor is overdue by running a feature called "Your Period: The Real Deal." The information presented is accurate, straightforward, and helpful. But it's interspersed with five menstrual product ads that reinforce the readers' insecurities about bleeding, reminding them about "embarrassing leaks," "soggy-mess-of-a-pad[s]," and "odors.")

Indeed, the very structure of these magazines reflects this dichotomy by formally dividing different aspects of self into separate sections. Mary Cantwell, writing about *Mademoiselle* during the 1950s, says the editors described themselves as either "visual" or "verbal," meaning that different editors attended to different aspects of the reader's self.[55] While women's magazines have a long tradition of compartmentalizing body and self, today's girls feel the pinch—the difficulty of integrating the two—at the intersection of sex.

Girls may find it particularly difficult to conceptualize sex the way the magazines present it, as an either/or event—one that satisfies either the body or the self—since they are used to the more integrated approach of childhood, when their bodies and their sensations were themselves. They are simultaneously perplexed about why sex, or more specifically desire, and menstruation seem to share the same concealment taboos. The teen magazines, reflecting adult notions of what is in a girl's best interest, do their best to hit readers over the head with these rules without shedding a lot of light on their origins.

Girls learn that, aside from their basic biology, sex and menstruation are linked under the heading of "Naughty." Menstruation announces to the world that you're a sexual being, and the world denounces your sexuality. When it comes to sex, the message in teen magazines today is ancient and proscriptive—good girls don't—but in the wake of feminism and the sexual revolution, the message has been repackaged as *choice*. Do whatever you wanna do, editors and writers tell the girls, but I betcha you'll be sorry afterwards. The new demon is "emotional distress."

For example, in one of its July 1997 advice columns, *Seventeen* riffs on the seduced-and-abandoned theme, then takes a gloomy detour into the perennially popular why-buy-the-cow-when-you-get-the-milk-for-free warning, reminding girls that their fellah might stop calling once he's gotten what he wants. Worse still, the unidentified writer warns, "What if you feel weird afterward, and even regret doing it?" One article in the January 1997 *Seventeen*, titled "Bad Reputation," is a four-page chronicle of one girl's fall from grace after "fooling around" with a guy who talked about it. Though the writer doesn't specify that "fooling around" meant intercourse, saying instead that they "made out pretty seriously," her cautionary tale warns girls that "in the space of a few hours, I had become a 'slut.'"

In the ever-popular "Ten Guys to Avoid" articles—which are recycled almost annually in these magazines—the boy who wants sex always makes a cameo appearance and is always bad news. In the November 1995 *Teen*, he's labeled "the sex-centered guy." Warning girls that they need to "understand the consequences of [their] actions," the writer paints a grim picture, citing the emotional dangers of abandonment and the physical dangers of pregnancy and sexually transmitted diseases. A 1995 Miss Teenage America finalist recites "The ABCs of Abstinence" in the December 1995 *Teen*. For each letter of the alphabet, she presents a reason why "sex is uncool and being a virgin is smart." The almost–beauty queen, laboring under her clunky structural conceit, squeezes this in under 'K': "Knowledge is key. Learn about the possible physical and emotional consequences of having sex before you're ready." An article in the November 1994 *Teen* with the misleading title

"Sexual Choices: Should You Wait?" is a three-page diatribe by the Reverend Jerry Melson, who peddles abstinence via the Religious Right's "True Love Waits" program. (Teens who have already succumbed to temptation are introduced to the term "second virginity" and reminded that "anyone, virgin or not, can decide to begin now to abstain from sex until they are married.")

Combing through five years of these magazines, I never encountered a single reference to a girl who wanted to have sex simply because she thought sex might feel good. Every single advice column assumed girls were being pressured by boys and their peers and warned wavering virgins to wait. Sex is described passively as "losing your virginity." Teenage girls learn all about sex from these magazines, and they discover that it is about boys' bodies liking girls' bodies to the detriment of girls' selves. A misguided teen who might confuse suggestions that she be an object of desire with permission to do the desiring is quickly set straight.

Wayward girls beware, the magazines warn. In a typical morality tale, this one appearing in the August 1995 *Teen*, a "true story" is titled "He Only Wanted Me for Sex." In it, Brittany has sex with Tad and then regrets it. In a major way. "Whenever I think back on all that's happened, I feel these waves of grief," Brittany says as the story opens. "Like someone died or something. And I want to go back and try to fix it, change the whole story so that it has a different ending. I used to pray that I'd wake up and be my old self again." When I read this dramatic opening, I assumed this was a story about date rape. But as Brittany backs up to the beginning, readers learn that she merely had intercourse with her boyfriend. In describing the event, Brittany portrays herself passively—or the ghost-writer or the magazine editors do—because . . . well, good girls are passive, right? "I still wasn't going to *give in* [my italics]. But then he said I was beautiful," Brittany explains. Later, she anticipates Ellen Fein and Sherrie Schneider's advice book *The Rules*,[56] which itself borrows from a host of moralists dating back to at least the 1700s. Brittany writes:

> I think maybe he was surprised that I had given in to him, even though that's what he wanted. I think maybe he liked the challenge of trying to get me to have sex more than he liked actually having sex. And I guess I wasn't much of a challenge anyway, so he sort of lost interest."

This is the kind of story that girls (six million of them, according to circulation figures[57]) read as they grapple with puberty and struggle to make sense of their changing bodies and their changing place in the world. Now, given that *Seventeen*—and *YM* and *Teen*—has a readership that is clearly younger than seventeen, its suggestions that young girls need the confidence to resist sexual pressure make some sense. But if thirteen-, fourteen-, and fifteen-year-olds are the ones gobbling up these magazines, their instructional role becomes even more pivotal. Indeed, a 1997 Kaiser Family Foundation survey discovered that 7 out of 10 girls aged thirteen to eighteen regularly read the top teen magazines, *YM*, *Seventeen*, and *Teen*. Of the teens surveyed, 51 percent said they relied on the magazines for information about sex and 69 percent said this was information that they didn't get from other sources.[58]

When it came to sex, most of them didn't even have enough experience to apply against hyperbole.

By the time a girl graduates to women's magazines like *Cosmopolitan* or *Redbook,* articles that tell her how to attract or sexually satisfy her man will alternate with articles that try to undo the damage of the former—and the teen magazines she used to read—by telling her to trust her desire, make her wants known, and, for chrissakes, just relax in bed. According to the Kaiser Family Foundation survey, which looked at the top women's magazines, 34 percent of the articles on sex focused on technique, 28 percent on sex appeal, and 16 percent on sexual fantasies.[59] Teenage girls got a different dose of information: 50 percent of the teen magazine articles on sex were of the should-I-or-shouldn't-I variety; 23 percent mused on virginity; and 20 percent discussed rape, sexual abuse, or incest. Sexually transmitted diseases, unintended pregnancy, or HIV and AIDS were mentioned in 57 percent of the teen magazine articles on sex.

What happens to a girl who reads only tired, didactic stories about all the bad things that will happen to her if she has sex? What does she do after ingesting all these articles and pictures and fashion spreads that equate beauty and power with those who control their fat, their pimples, their bulges? Which portray her body as an enemy she must control at a time when her body seems so out of control? What does it mean for her to sift through the rhetoric in order to understand what sex and desire have in common with blood and cum? Because the shared code of silence surrounding them implies connection. What's a fourteen-year-old to make of all this?

As a grownup, *I* couldn't figure it all out. Everything I read in these magazines told me that the taboos surrounding desire and menstruation were linked—both events take place "down there," and "down there" is nasty—but there was a synapse lapse when I tried to carry it further. Why are the two linked and why are both *bad?* Logically, menstruation in girls should be greeted joyfully by a culture that pushes abstinence, interpreted as proof a girl is still treading the straight and narrow (i.e., not pregnant). It didn't make sense.

Then I had an epiphany: it didn't make sense because it was utterly illogical.

When I was sixteen, my best friend, D.J., and I were on a long, long train ride. We had hours to kill and we were bored. We were talking about boys and then sex and then gender inequities, except we didn't call them that because neither of us had the vocabulary for a problem that we were only beginning to sense. I still have the little blue Mead memo notebook we wrote in.

Because D.J. and I were taking geometry, and because we thought we were terribly clever and funny, we laid out our observations of the world around us as "theorems" and "postulates." Theorem I is titled "Male vs. Female" and is defined as "Theory that ponders and debates [this last word is crossed out and the word "protests" is penciled in] the vast differences between two sexes of the same species, probes into their specified roles and peculiar behavior." Beneath that, our Postulate I is a riff on "the macho-man." We note how men feel the "need to be the strong ones, the cool ones, the unemotional ones, the top bananas in our society." Postulate II, labelled "Stud vs. Slut," further describes the rules as we see them:

> When a young male has his first sexual encounter he feels the need to spew the gory details, tell every guy in town, whereas a female, after losing her virginity is in-clinded [*sic*] to be embarassed [*sic*], hushed mouthed, and maybe even guilty. This brings to light the situation wherein the male who fucks every Mary, Jane, and Sue, people tend to chuckle, saying, "He's quite the young studly type." However, the female who engages in similar activities with every Tom, Dick (no pun intended), and Harry is alienated, called a shameless hussy, and shunned by her peers (of both sexes) . . .

We persist with our little three-by-five-inch document. We are spoofing geometry, but we're also hopeful that in organizing our observations via this exact science based on if-then logic, the rules, which are beginning to come into focus, won't seem so confusing and contradictory. Giggling, we continue.

By our third postulate, we eschew the neutral language of science in favor of agitprop. Because, by now, we're indignant. We take on desire:

> We wish to denounce the widely held oppinion [*sic*] that women lack the intense sexual drive that males undoubt-edly posess [*sic*]. Because of this belief, women have been tricked into suppressing their own full bodied sexual de-sires. This leads to inhibitions and abnormal suppressions in women today.

Two more "postulates" deal with double standards regarding masturbation and beauty. Then we give up. It's gotten too complicated for us to pursue.

The notebook is my coming-of-age story. I remember writing it. I remember sweltering on the train. I remember pausing to eat tuna, directly out of a can, because we were scrimping on our trip's food allowance so we could buy clothes. I remember the relish we took in coming up with multisyllabic words — adult words, formal words — to give our ideas weight. I remember the deliciously "naughty" pleasure we took in coming up with phrases like "full bodied sexual desires." And I remember the euphoria. I was happy because my best friend saw things the way I did. And I thought, for the first time, maybe I wasn't crazy after all.

A Hygienic Crisis

The notebook is a tangible, tiny, cryptic fragment of my adolescence. It freeze-frames a moment when I first poked my head out of the confused, dark tunnel I now recognize as puberty. D.J. and I, who at sixteen were first articulating the catch-22 we found ourselves in, believed we were the first girls in the world to discover and document these differing expectations.

We were more typical than we knew.

Experts at the Society for Menstrual Cycle Research — a maverick band of mostly women academics who conduct and encourage research on the topic — have evidence indicating that menarche precipitates a "hygienic crisis" among many girls. In the past few years there's been a flurry of attention devoted to adolescent girls and the crisis in confidence they encounter at puberty. Carol Gilligan, a psychologist and author of *In a*

Different Voice, made headlines in 1982 with a study showing that girls use a system of moral reasoning that is not acknowledged, or honored, by the larger culture, and that they are in danger of losing their confidence and voices as a result. In 1991, the American Association of University Women published the results of a national survey, *Shortchanging Girls, Shortchanging America*, a report showing that somewhere along the way to adolescence girls lose their self-esteem. Peggy Orenstein, whose 1994 book *School Girls: Young Women, Self-Esteem, and the Confidence Gap* is based on the AAUW study, interviews dozens of girls at two schools in California: the book is a fascinating testament to the fact that sexism is alive and well and particularly debilitating for young girls on the precipice of puberty.[60] More recently, Mary Pipher's 1994 book *Reviving Ophelia: Saving the Selves of Adolescent Girls* made waves with its similar, though less energetic, call to arms. Pipher warns parents that depression, anorexia, and bulimia are only the most serious outward signs of a crisis many girls are facing as they struggle to finesse puberty in a sexist culture.[61]

The trigger, researchers think, may be menstruation. According to Mental Health Department statistics gathered in 1989 in the United States, New Zealand, Canada, and Puerto Rico, the likelihood of severe depression doubles for girls in the year after the onset of menstruation.[62] While Gilligan, Orenstein, and Pipher document the changes a girl gradually goes through as she discovers that her place in the world is different from that of the boys she chums around with, studies gathered by the Society for Menstrual Cycle Research suggest that transformation, or an identity crisis, may be jump-started by menarche.

Dr. Sharon Golub, past president of the Society for Menstrual Cycle Research, the editor of two books on menstruation, and a recognized expert on the topic, compiled the findings of much of the existing menstrual research in her 1992 book *Periods*. There Golub notes that while the physical changes girls go through in puberty happen slowly, when they get their periods, they suddenly have a different body image. (Some studies published by the society indicate that, in fact, people immediately perceive a girl who has begun to menstruate as being different, and that girls are treated differently once they've started menstruating. For example, parents' expectations change, dating is permitted, makeup is encouraged, etc.) "[Girls] apparently reorganize their body images in the direction of greater sexual maturity," Golub explains. "They are more mature. However, they are also more self-conscious, embarrassed, and secretive about their bodies." In one 1983 study, researchers asked seventh-grade girls to draw a male and a female. Girls who were premenarchal, regardless of what they actually looked like themselves, drew slim, bustless, hipless women dressed in fairly gender-neutral clothes. When the interviewer returned six months later and repeated the request, girls who had since started menstruating drew radically different pictures. Their females suddenly had breasts and hips, wore jewelry or heels, and, in one picture, carried a bouquet of flowers. The pictures reflected a newfound awareness of a more "feminine" body and a new attention to appearance. They had changed.[63]

If menstruation is a crystallizing event, putting girls firmly in the women's camp, as de Beauvoir suggests, how do girls cope with their new bodies? And the way folks treat them now? They think it's a bummer.

One woman, recalling her first period on the Red Spot Web site (redspot@onewoman.com), put it quite succinctly:

> I was 13 when it started. I don't remember where. I told my mom, and she gave me the line "Now you're a woman." I thought "Oh, great. Why me?"

Her anecdote jibes with the facts. Golub writes about a 1984 study of 205 girls in grades 6 through 10 that discovered a link between menarche and girls' feelings of self-esteem, depression, and sense of ability to control their lives. "The girls who were postmenarcheal for less than two years had the lowest self-esteem scores and the highest scores on the measure of depressive mood," she explains. "By contrast, the girls who were more than two years postmenarcheal had the highest self-esteem scores and the lowest depressive affect scores." In another study of young girls, psychiatric epidemiologist Patricia Cohen found that severe depression peaked in girls who were thirteen or fourteen, soon after the onset of menstruation.[64]

It is easy to see how the crisis in confidence that is described by Gilligan, the AAUW, Orenstein, and Pipher might be precipitated by the arrival of menstruation. Your period is irrefutable proof that you're a woman, and just when you sense that the rules of the game are different and you'd like to sit back to quietly figure out how you fit, your body—larger breasts, bigger hips, leaking vagina—threatens to betray you by attracting attention to you. The "hygienic crisis" that researchers at the Society for Menstrual Research have discovered means that girls see menarche as a turning point. If the onset of menstruation bridges the gap between girls and women, are teens resisting the implications? And if so, why?

———

In my little blue Mead memo notebook, D.J. and I have obviously grown frustrated by our efforts to explain what makes us mad. We just know we are. We abandon our theorems and postulates in favor of a list. We call it "Hateful Words," and it consists of the following entries: "basically," "adolescent," "teenager," "menstruation," "pimple," "acne," "date," "girls & boys," "mature (pronounced ma-tour, ugh!)," "nice," and "nice girls." It reads as an indictment of puberty.

LITERATURE AND THE MENSTRUAL CANON

Back at camp, ten-year-old Rebecca is still fretting about this mysterious thing called "periods." Having learned, to her great relief, that she probably has a year before it hits her, she now worries about its duration. "How long do you have your period for?" she wants to know.

Missy, the resident expert, thinks for a moment and then answers. "My grandmother just stopped hers and she's sixty."

"Omigod! Her grandmother just stopped and she's sixty?" Sandra asks. She looks at me for confirmation.

"Till around then. Fifty. Maybe sixty," I say.

"Every day?" Rebecca asks.

"Once a month," Missy corrects.

"The bad thing about periods is you have to buy those . . . things," Sandra interjects.

"You can just use toilet paper," Missy tells her. "Gretchen just used a washcloth in her pants." She goes on to tell a long, detailed story about a girl named Gretchen who got her first period at home and had to temporarily wad up toilet paper in her underpants because her mom, a tampon user, didn't have any pads around. "It wasn't perfect, but it worked," Missy says.

"Who's Gretchen?" I wonder, assuming it's a fellow camper or classmate. Maybe I could interview her?

"Gretchen, in *Are You There God? It's Me, Margaret*," Missy says. "I read that book so many times." Missy explains that her mom bought it for her, even though she didn't want her to—at first. "When she told me what it was about, I said, 'Don't get it for me.' But she did anyway. Then I read it so many times." She smiles, sheepishly. "It was better than I thought."

Am I Normal? Judy Blume's Are You There God?

In all of the girl-lit canon, there is only one book where menstruation is central. Judy Blume's *Are You There God? It's Me, Margaret*, first published in 1972, is the dog-eared bible of the prepubescent set.[65] It is the fifth-best-selling kids' paperback of all time, with more than six million copies sold.[66] And in all of children's literature, *Are You There God?* is the eighth-best-selling book of all time.[67]

The 149-page book tells a modest story. It stars eleven-year-old Margaret, who has just moved from New York City to New Jersey. As the sixth-grader struggles with puberty and religion (her new friends want to know whether she'll join the Y or the Jewish Community Center, and Margaret's agnostic parents are disinclined to do either), she has daily chats with God. "Are you there God? It's me, Margaret," she begins each prayer, as if leaving an answering machine message for someone she hopes will pick up.

Shortly after Margaret arrives in the suburbs, a neighborhood girl invites her to join a club called the PTS's (Pre-Teen Sensations). Margaret is delighted until she learns the club's rules. Rule number one: girls in the club have to wear bras. (Margaret has no breasts, and therefore no bras.) Rule number two: girls in the club have to give an immediate and detailed account of their first period . . . when they get it. (Margaret frets that if she's lagging *this* far behind in the bosom department, it'll be years before she menstruates.) She takes her breast request to a higher power: "Please let me grow, God. You know where. I want to be like everyone else."

As the story proceeds, Margaret and her chums have a few menstrual adventures. They work up their nerve to buy pads at the drugstore so they can practice wearing them; they watch the requisite industry-sponsored menstrual flick in school ("It was like one big commercial," Margaret observes), and they trade period stories ("Well, I was sitting there eating my supper when I felt like something was dripping from me").

Later, when two of the four Pre-Teen Sensations have started menstruating, Margaret says a period prayer: "If I'm the last [to get my period] I don't know what I'll do," she says. "Oh please God. I just want to be normal." God grants her her wish. She bleeds, she graduates from sixth grade, and the story ends.

Are You There God? has never gotten the kind of widespread critical acclaim that popular children's books tend to elicit from librarians, teachers, and parents. Indeed, it is something of an anomaly in the field. As Mark Oppenheimer points out in a November 16, 1997, essay in *The New York Times*, "Why Judy Blume Endures," children's books that are successful are usually successful across the board—with committees giving out awards and librarians then purchasing and recommending the books to teachers, who give them to children to read. "The formula just did not work for [Blume]," Oppenheimer writes. "Her books never won awards, and teachers never assigned her books. But when I got to college, there was no author except Shakespeare whom more of my peers had read."

Among the kid-lit literati—adults—Blume's popularity is often dismissed as an aberration. Critics like Michele Landsberg and Davis Rees say that Blume is a "trivial" writer. They criticize her "flat, sloppy, ungrammatical, and inexpressive speech," describing her values as conventional and her realism as inappropriate for young-adult novels.

It's true that there is nothing extraordinary about *Are You There God?* in terms of literary merit. The language is not particularly lovely or evocative; the plot takes few surprising turns. Unlike, say, Louise Fitzhugh's books (*Harriet the Spy, Nobody's Family Is Going to Change*, etc.), where the characters have a moral agenda and are slightly larger than life, Blume's kids are so average they're almost boring.

But Blume's genius lies in her willingness to meet kids on

their own terms. Choosing to write about topics like divorce, teen sex, sibling rivalry, and menstruation in her books, Blume makes the array of conflicting emotions surrounding them acceptable. What adults would dismiss as trivial, Blume elevates. For example, *Are You There God?* takes girls' curiosity about menstruation seriously by talking about what it feels like to menstruate. According to Golub, author of *Periods* and past president of the Society for Menstrual Cycle Research, young girls often feel that biological explanations of menstruation are inadequate.[68] *Ovulation, egg, fallopian tube,* and *uterus* are abstract concepts to young girls, who wonder what it feels like to have blood come out of your vagina. Does it drip one drop at a time? Or does it rush like a river? (One ten-year-old camper I interviewed asked me why women had to wear pads day after day. "How come you can't just sit on the toilet and pee the blood out when it comes?" she wondered.) Blume captures this desire for the experiential aspects of bleeding in a scene where Gretchen, the first of the Pre-Teen Sensations to get her period, seems to be withholding the essence of the event from the others. "My mother showed me how to attach the pad to the belt. Oh . . . you know," Gretchen says. But her friends feel cheated. "Look, Gretchen, did we or did we not make a deal to tell each other absolutely everything about getting it?" one girl, Nancy, demands. But when Gretchen says, "I'm telling you, aren't I?" Nancy counters, "Not enough." She wants to know: "What's it feel like?"

The Pre-Teen Sensations want to know what it feels like so that they can anticipate the experience—which is one way of exerting limited control over their unpredictable bodies—and they want to check Gretchen's experiences against their own, just as readers use the characters' feelings as a barometer of their own normalcy. Young readers, like old readers, look for affirmation of the self in novels. To a young girl, if nobody talks about something—like menstruation or sex—in the real world, and yet she thinks about it, then she's convinced she's weird. But Margaret and her friends worry about the same things the reader does. So, yes, Blume is a conventional, even conservative, author, because her characters strive for normalcy. But what realists like Judy Blume, S. E. Hinton, Paul Zindel, and even J. D. Salinger do is take kids' feelings seriously, and *that* is still a radical move.

Indeed, Blume's books—including *Are You There God?*—have often been censored by parents and school boards, making them regulars on the American Library Association's annual list of most-challenged books. What is so threatening about *Are You There God?* that parents would storm PTA and school-board meetings to demand that it be pulled from the library shelves? Blume's convention-flouting book simply moves periods from the private realm into the public. That subversive act makes everybody nervous.

Power in the Blood: Stephen King's Carrie

And then there's Stephen King's *Carrie*, the creep-out girl who bled, wept, then made others bleed. Written for adults, *Carrie* is devoured by teens. It's the novel we read in high school to give ourselves the heebie-jeebies. The tattered copy we passed around to friends, the title page dripping with blood. The movie and the shower-room scene of Sissy Spacek being beaned by tampons that lingers with us still.

Here's a refresher on the plot.

Carrie is a social misfit who exudes vulnerability. Her high-school classmates sense that they can attack her relentlessly without fear of retribution. "She was a chunky girl with pimples on her neck and back and buttocks, her hair completely without color," King writes. "She looked the part of the sacrificial goat, the constant butt, believer in left-handed monkey wrenches, perpetual foul-up, and she was."

Everybody is mean to Carrie. Her growing-up years are grim:

There had been all these years, all these years of let's short-sheet Carrie's bed at Christian Youth Camp and I found this love letter from Carrie to Flash Bobby Pickett let's copy it and pass it around and hide her underpants somewhere and put this snake in her shoe and duck her *again*, duck her *again* . . .[69]

The barrage of tricks peaks in Carrie's senior year of high school. Then, King writes, "the ultimate shit-on, gross-out, put-down, long searched for, was found." Carrie menstruates. Publicly.

She gets her first period one day while showering after gym, and because her mom is a religious fanatic who quite literally believes this "curse" is visited only upon sinners—and her daughter surely ain't one—Carrie knows nothing about it. When Carrie's classmates see her standing there, wet, naked, and bleeding, the ensuing shower-room scene is brutal:

"Per-iod!"
The catcall came first from Chris Hargensen. It struck the tiled walls, rebounded, and struck again. Sue Snell

gasped laughter from her nose and felt an odd, vexing mixture of hate, revulsion, exasperation, and pity. She just looked so *dumb,* standing there, not knowing what was going on. God, you'd think she never—

"PER-iod!"

It was becoming a chant, an incantation. Someone in the background (perhaps Hargensen again, Sue couldn't tell in the jungle of echoes) was yelling, *"Plug it up!"* with hoarse, uninhibited abandon . . .

"You're *bleeding!"* Sue yelled suddenly, furiously. "You're *bleeding,* you big dumb pudding!"

. . . Then the laughter, disgusted, contemptuous, horrified, seemed to rise and bloom into something jagged and ugly, and the girls were bombarding her with tampons and sanitary napkins, some from purses, some from the broken dispenser on the wall. They flew like snow and the chant became: "Plug it *up,* plug it *up,* plug it *up,* plug it—"[70]

The hatefest is interrupted by the P.E. teacher, who has to struggle to control her own revulsion at the sight of Carrie. She chastises the other girls and sends Carrie home to recuperate.

But in this odd coming-of-age novel, Carrie's menarche is linked to a surge in her hitherto latent telekinetic powers. As Carrie bleeds, she connects with her inner power. Suddenly she can move objects—hairbrushes, chairs, beds—with her mind.

Fast-forward 150 pages and Carrie has been invited to the senior prom. As a joke, her classmates vote her prom queen, lure her onto the stage, and then dump two bucketfuls of pigs' blood on her head. Carrie's classmates have crossed her line in the sand. Her stress-related telekinetic powers go into high gear. Her fantasies of retaliation become reality. All hell breaks loose. She flees the streamer-decorated gymnasium, telekinetically locks all the doors to the high school, and starts a fire. She burns up all of her classmates, destroys most of her hometown, and then kills her mother, the disturbed zealot whom she blames for her misfit status. Exhausted, she dies herself from the strain such herculean telekinetic tasks have put on her body. The end.

Carrie was originally published without a title or even King's name on the cover. Instead, the cover read simply, "A novel of a girl possessed of a terrifying power."[71] The first print run was for 700,000 copies. Within nine months, 1.33 million copies of the book had been sold. Today there are four million copies of *Carrie* in print. Toss in a pass-along value of one—each reader gives it to a friend—and the millions who saw Brian DePalma's 1976 film version of the book and there are more people with *Carrie* floating around in their subconscious than there are residents of New York City.

Carrie clearly struck a chord. Now, in the menstrual-lit loop—in publications by the Society for Menstrual Cycle Research and in the smattering of books and academic essays on the topic—critiques of *Carrie* surface with some regularity. Usually King is dismissed as a misogynist. Who else would connect menstruation with a mean streak a mile wide?

But, I don't think it's that simple. In *Carrie*, King did what he does best. He took our tiny fears—careful when you pass that standpipe, walk over a subway grate, house-sit for a stranger—and magnified them. A lot.

King's talent lies in his ability to tap our fears. Whose fears, though? Boys'? Or girls'? In my high school, boys and girls both gobbled up this book. But for different reasons. Boys read it because it plays into latent fears about the mysteries of menstruation and its connection to power and sexuality. But girls get a different thrill. We read it both because we remember being *that* mean to our school's version of Carrie and because we've either been a Carrie ourselves or have precariously balanced on the edge of Carrie-dom; we revel in the revenge fantasies the novel provides. This girl gets back at her enemies.

The vengeance is delicious because the agony—in teen vernacular—is so well drawn. The book draws to a close on prom night. Carrie is at the prom with one of the cutest, most popular boys in the school. She is about to be crowned prom queen. And, stranger than anything, everybody is actually being nice to her for the first time.

When Carrie falls, she falls doubly hard because, just for a moment, she dares to hope. But like most teenage girls, she doubts her likability, viewing her classmates' admiration as fickle and transitory. And, in this horror story, it is.

With a chilling, there-but-for-the-grace-of-God feeling, readers watch in dismay as approval for Carrie turns quickly to derision—with the help of two bucketfuls of pigs' blood. King writes:

> They had taken her again, gulled her again, made her the butt again, . . . they had gotten her up here, up here in front of the whole school, and had repeated the shower-room scene . . . only the voice had said

(my god that's blood)

something too awful to be contemplated. If she opened her eyes and it was true, oh, what then? What then?

. . . The final nightmare, she was red and dripping with it, they had drenched her in the very secretness of blood, in front of all of them and her thought

(oh . . . i . . . COVERED . . . with it)

was colored a ghastly purple with her revulsion and her shame. She could smell herself and it was the stink of blood, the awful wet, coppery smell. In a flickering kaleidoscope of images she saw the blood running thickly down her naked thighs, heard the constant beating of the shower on the tiles, felt the soft patter of tampons and napkins against her skin as voices exhorted her to plug it up, tasted the plump, fulsome bitterness of horror. They had finally given her the shower they wanted.[72]

But—and this is where the *real* appeal is for girl readers— Carrie is not defeated. She gets mad. And even.

Carrie converts a liability (menstruation, or becoming a woman) into an asset (power, more specifically the power to destroy, a decidedly unfeminine and unnurturing fantasy). Girls get a vicarious thrill from Carrie, Combative and Triumphant Destroyer of Tormentors.

A Girl's Own Story: Anne Frank

Carrie is a striking departure from the traditional canon of prepubescent literature—all the books girls read when they are on the edge of adolescence. From *Elsie Dinsmore* to *Heidi*, from

Pollyanna to all the "littles" (*Little House on the Prairie, Little Women, A Little Princess*) these classics-for-girls preach another response to adversity: submission.

But what happens when a girl writes about her own life, contemporaneously? Plenty of girls do, in their diaries, but the writing is rarely skillful enough or the subject interesting enough to merit publication. The most famous exception, of course, is *Anne Frank: The Diary of a Young Girl*.

Anne Frank's diary has been the subject of some controversy lately. Originally published in 1947 by Otto Frank, Anne's father and the only surviving member of the Secret Annexe where eight Jews spent more than two years of World War II in hiding, the diary was reissued in 1995.[73] Included in this new edition were passages that Otto Frank had deleted from the original edition. Apparently, in the process of trimming the journal to fit the specifications of a Dutch publisher, Frank had "cleaned up" the diary, eliminating some of Anne's biting comments about her friends and her mother, some of her musings about sex, and some passages about her faith.

In 1997, not long after Doubleday's "definitive edition" of *Anne Frank* hit bookstores, a new Broadway play based on the diary opened. Simultaneously, two books—Lawrence Graver's *An Obsession with Anne Frank: Meyer Levin and the Diary* and Ralph Melnick's *The Stolen Legacy of Anne Frank: Meyer Levin, Lillian Hellman, and the Staging of the Diary*—were published. This sparked a flurry of interest in Anne Frank. *The New Yorker, Time, The New Republic*, and *Vogue* all checked in on the topic. Writers and critics revisited the 1955 Broadway show based on the diary, the 1958 movie based on the diary, the original diary, the revised diary, the books about the diary, all in an effort to determine whose interpretation of the diary should prevail. In a fascinating *New Yorker* article (October 6, 1997), Cynthia Ozick criticized all the "interpretations" of *Anne Frank* for mistakenly emphasizing her girlish optimism. Acknowledging that the diary is "miraculous, a self-aware work of youthful genius," Ozick goes on to say that the public's tendency to focus on the diary's most celebrated line—"I still believe, in spite of everything, that people are truly good at heart"—is a perversion of the facts. She also argues that viewing the book as an adolescent classic is an ahistorical and dangerously wrongheaded way of interpreting the diary. Anyone who suggests that Anne Frank's legacy is to "the children of the world" is dismissed for having "reduced the persecution of a people to the trials of adolescence."[74]

And yet young girls all over the world seem to have claimed the diary for their own. It belongs to their canon. English teachers put it on reading lists, bookstores place it in the "Young Adults" section, and those of us who read it as girls recommend it to other girls. We think they'd like it, because as young girls we liked it. Though as grown-ups we're hard-pressed to explain why. Our memories of the diary are vague. We recall the big picture, the plot: during World War II Anne Frank spent more than two years hiding in a cramped attic with her family and another family before being discovered by the police and ultimately sent to Bergen-Belsen, where she died at the hands of the Nazis. But we have lost track of the details of Anne's adolescent life.

And yet the details form a sizable portion of the diary. Because of Anne's confinement and all the time she had on her hands, she digs deeply into her psyche and minutely records what is often dismissed as the trivia of adolescence. Immersed in the throes of adolescent passion, Anne takes her feelings seriously. This speaks to girls.

Why is that?

As an adult rereading *Anne Frank*, I initially found myself impatient with her adolescent angst: her arguments with her mother, her endless analysis of her personality, her defense of her own virtues and subsequent chastisement of herself, and finally her self-flagellating desire to be "good." In other words, all the mundane elements of this book that make it not unlike my own diary—or the thousands of angst-filled girlish diaries hidden in boxes in aging parents' basements across the country. What interests me, I *thought*, as I read this, were the extraordinary aspects of the story: what made Anne Frank's experience specific, and different from that of white Catholic girls like myself who grew up safe, fed, and warm in 1970s America.

But why was I annoyed with Anne's typical-teenage-ness, the familiar and the predictable? I returned to the diary, this time reading it for the girlish elements, the love story and the anger toward her parents, the typical touchstones of adolescence which Anne experienced despite her unique historical circumstance. A girl becomes a woman in the course of the diary, and the journey, meticulously documented, is revealing.

On October 29, 1942, Anne writes that she is "allowed to read more grown-up books lately." Referring to a love story called *Eva's Youth*, she notes that "Eva has a monthly period." Anne's excited at the prospect. "Oh, I'm so longing to have it too; it seems so important." (The word *longing*, so dramatic and yet apt for the depth of feeling she is struggling to define, is a favorite of Anne's.)

A few days later she adds a postscript to her entry:

> I forgot to mention the important news that I'm probably going to get my period soon. I can tell because I keep finding a whitish smear in my panties, and Mother predicted it would start soon. I can hardly wait. It's such a momentous event. Too bad I can't use sanitary napkins, but you can't get them anymore, and Mama's tampons can be used only by women who've had a baby.[75]

In fact, the whitish discharge is a false alarm and she doesn't get her period for some time. Oddly enough, she doesn't note down the actual day she starts. Instead, she mentions her period in passing on January 5, 1944: "Each time I have a period—and that has only been three times—I have the feeling that in spite of all the pain, unpleasantness, and nastiness, I have a sweet secret, and that is why, although it is nothing but a nuisance to me in a way, I always long for the time that I shall feel that secret within me again."[76] For now, Anne's entrée into womanhood thrills her. Still, she is well versed in the clandestine nature of the event. "I think what is happening to me is so wonderful, and not only what can be seen on my body, but all that is taking place inside," she writes in the same entry. "I never discuss myself or any of these things with anybody; that is why I have to talk to myself about them." In the remarkably forthright passage that follows, she goes on to do just that:

> After I came here, when I was just fourteen, I began to think about myself sooner than most girls, and to know that I am a "person." Sometimes, when I lie in bed at

night, I have a terrible desire to feel my breasts and to listen to the quiet rhythmic beat of my heart.

I already had these kinds of feelings subconsciously before I came here, because I remember that once when I slept with a girl friend I had a strong desire to kiss her, and that I did do so. I could not help being terribly inquisitive over her body, for she had always kept it hidden from me. I asked her whether, as proof of our friendship, we should feel one another's breasts, but she refused. I go into ecstasies every time I see the naked figure of a woman, such as Venus, for example. It strikes me as so wonderful and exquisite that I have difficulty in stopping the tears rolling down my cheeks.

If only I had a girl friend!

Yours, Anne[77]

(The very next entry reads almost as a correction. "My *longing* to talk to someone became so intense that somehow or other I took it into my head to choose Peter," she writes, referring to the Secret Annexe's only teenage boy.) It doesn't take long before Anne begins to puzzle over why something that she finds kind of "wonderful"—like her changing body—is dealt with so furtively. By the time she has had her period four, maybe five, times, she begins to wonder why periods—or anything to do with "down there"—is something nice girls don't talk about.

On January 24, 1944, she writes: "Before I came here, whenever anyone at home or at school talked about sex, they were either secretive or disgusting. Any words having to do with sex were spoken in a low whisper, and kids who weren't in the know were often laughed at. That struck me as odd, and I often wondered why people were so mysterious or obnoxious when they talked about this subject." She hadn't questioned this then. "Mother once said to me, 'Anne, let me give you some good advice. Never discuss this with boys, and if they bring it up, don't answer them.' I still remember my exact reply. 'No, of course not,' I exclaimed. 'Imagine!' And nothing more was said."[78] What pushes Anne to question the wisdom of her mother's words is an incident with Peter and a cat who shares the Annexe with them. Trying to determine the cat's sex, Peter flips it onto its back. "If any other boy had pointed out the 'male sexual organ' to me, I would never have given him a second glance. But Peter went on talking in a normal voice about what is otherwise a very awkward subject . . . I felt so much at ease that I started acting normally too."[79] Anne is beginning to make her first forays into the minefield of sexual etiquette, and she is trying to make sense of the seemingly senseless rules that govern such interactions. In a diary entry dated March 18, 1944, she again delves into the topic:

Parents and people in general, are very peculiar when it comes to sex. Instead of telling their sons and daughters everything at the age of twelve, they send the children out of the room the moment the subject arises and leave them to find out everything on their own . . . Soon after I turned eleven, they told me about menstruation. But even then, I had no idea where the blood came from or what it was for. When I was twelve and a half, I learned some more from Jacque [a girlfriend], who wasn't as ignorant as I was. My own intuition told me what a man and a woman do when they're together; it seemed like a crazy idea at first, but when Jacque confirmed it, I was proud of myself for having figured it out! . . . I also knew that you could keep from having children, but how that worked inside your body remained a mystery . . .

If mothers don't tell their children everything, they hear it in bits and pieces, and that can't be right.[80]

For the next few days, Anne and Peter trade bits of information. He tells her how birth control works, and she tells him what girls' genitals look like. But first, in a disarmingly frank journal entry, she plans out her description. She begins by musing about whether Peter "knows what girls look like down there," and observes that she doesn't think "boys are as complicated as girls" in this regard. Then she gives herself a thorough inspection—which includes sticking her finger in her vagina. Not surprisingly, this is one of the passages edited out of the original *Anne Frank*. The passage—which I'll quote at length because it creates such a vivid image of Anne on her Annexe cot with a mirror in her hand—reads:

How on earth can you explain what it all looks like without any models? Shall I try anyway? Okay, here goes!

When you're standing up, all you see from the front is hair. Between your legs there are two soft, cushiony things, also covered with hair, which press together when you're standing, so you can't see what's inside. They separate when you sit down, and they're very red and quite fleshy on the inside. In the upper part, between the outer labia, there's a fold of skin that, on second thought, looks like a kind of blister. That's the clitoris. Then come the inner labia, which are also pressed together in a kind of crease. When they open up, you can see a fleshy little mound, no bigger than the top of my thumb. The upper part has a couple of small holes in it, which is where the urine comes out. The lower part looks as if it were just skin, and yet that's where the vagina is. You can barely find it, because the folds of skin hide the opening. The hole's so small I can hardly imagine how a man could get in there, much less how a baby could come out. It's hard enough trying to get your index finger inside. That's all there is, and yet it plays such an important role![81]

When it comes to sexuality and desire, Anne takes the step (unprecedented in girls' classics) of acknowledging hers. On January 12, 1944, she writes: "Once, when we spoke about sex, Daddy told me that I couldn't possibly understand the longing yet; I always knew that I did understand it and now I understand it fully."

Anne alternates between a straightforward sexual desire and the more acceptable desire for "romance." She pins her hopes on Peter, but it's a bit of a stretch for her; the more she gets to know him, the less interesting he turns out to be. ("Peter is good and he's a darling, but still there's no denying that there's a lot about him that disappoints me," she says on June 14, 1944.) He's not as smart as her, and he lacks her pluck and determination. This bothers Anne. Still, for a while, given her limited circle of Annexe dwellers he is the only possible romantic candidate (the only other one under fifty years of age is Anne's sister, Margot). And so she fantasizes about him. On February 13, 1944, she writes about her changing body:

I believe that it's spring within me, I feel that spring is awakening. I feel it in my whole body and soul. It is an effort to behave normally, I feel utterly confused, don't know what to read, what to write, what to do, I only know that I am longing . . . ![82]

The next day, she follows up with this:

Since Saturday a lot has changed for me. It came about like this. I longed—and am still longing—but . . . now something has happened, which has made it a little, just a little, less.

To my great joy—I will be quite honest about it—already this morning I noticed that Peter kept looking at me all the time. Not in the ordinary way, I don't know how, I just can't explain.[83]

By March 16, 1944, she is writing:

Thank goodness the others can't tell what my inward feelings are . . . I'm not so affectionate to Daddy and don't tell Margot a single thing. I'm completely closed up. Above all, I must maintain my outward reserve, no one must know that war still reigns incessantly within. War between desire and common sense.[84]

All of the preceding passages about sex and desire appear within the four months following Anne's announcement that she is menstruating. It's significant that another battle runs parallel to Anne's struggles with her changing body, her budding sexuality, and her subsequent efforts to pin down the rules regarding both. In this battle, "reigning incessantly within," Anne is growing up. Part of what she writes about—her separation from her parents and her growing independence—is textbook-variety adolescent development and could apply to either gender. But other aspects of Anne's struggle seem specific to girlhood. For example, Anne has a rough time trying to reconcile her parents' expectations of *woman*hood—as opposed to adulthood—with her own. Anne is looking for affirmation of her feelings and is devastated to discover she'll get none. This takes its toll.

In the diary's opening entries, a bravely self-confident girl notices that expectations about her behavior are changing. Navigating the new rules is trying, but hardly debilitating. In December 1942, a sassy and sarcastic twelve-year-old Anne complains about the grown-ups' expectations.

> Oh, I'm becoming so sensible! One must apply one's reason to everything here, learning to obey, to hold your tongue, to help, to be good, to give in, and I don't know what else. I'm afraid I shall use up all my brains too quickly, and I haven't got so very many. Then I shall not have any left for when the war is over.[85]

Less than a year later, on July 11, 1943, she learns that she'll have an easier time of things if she *pretends* to agree with the grown-ups:

I do really see that I get on better by shamming a bit, instead of my old habit of telling everyone exactly what I think . . .

I often lose my cue and simply can't swallow my rage at some injustice, so that for four long weeks we hear nothing but an everlasting chatter about the cheekiest and most shameless girl on earth.[86]

By March 7, 1944, a number of months after Anne has had her first period and in the midst of puzzling over the covert nature of periods and all things sexual, her confidence is crumbling. She begins to see all her "faults and shortcomings, which are so great" and decides that it is time to "face the difficult task of changing myself, to stop the everlasting reproaches, which were so oppressive and which reduced me to such terrible despondency." She is having a hard time. "I came to the conclusion that the others no longer had the right to throw me about like an india-rubber ball," she writes. "I wanted to change in accordance with my own desires." But it was difficult. At the end of this entry, she writes: "In due time I quieted down and discovered my boundless desire for all that is beautiful and good."[87] Later that month, she reasserts herself:

Although I am only fourteen, I know quite well what I want, I know who is right and who is wrong, I have my opinions, my own ideas and principles, and although it may sound pretty mad from an adolescent, I feel more of a person than a child, I feel quite independent of anyone.[88]

Clearly, Anne's circumstances have forced her to grow up quickly and made her hyperaware of personality-defining issues such as religion, morality, and politics. She is proud of her knowledge and opinions. At the same time, she is beginning to realize that woman's narrowly circumscribed role in the world will leave her little space to act on them. Is there a place for a cheeky, opinionated girl like herself? She struggles to visualize what her life and person might be like as she becomes a woman, and she resists the role models that are held out to her. She wants more for herself. On April 4, 1944, she writes:

I want to get on; I can't imagine that I would have to lead the same sort of life as Mummy and Mrs. Van Daan and all the women who do their work and are then forgotten. I must have something besides a husband and children, something that I can devote myself to![89]

Her mother's world, as she describes it on April 11, 1944, is decidedly unappealing to her:

I know what I want, I have a goal, an opinion, I have a religion and love. Let me be myself and then I am satisfied. I know that I'm a woman, a woman with inward strength and plenty of courage.

If God lets me live, I shall attain more than Mummy ever has done, I shall not remain insignificant, I shall work in the world and for mankind![90]

A few weeks later, though, the doubt returns. As things get hot and heavy in her romance with Peter (though they go only so far as kissing and cuddling), she grows confused about what she is *supposed* to feel. She wonders, "Is it right? Is it right for me to yield so soon, for me to be so passionate, to be filled with as much passion and desire as Peter? Can I, a girl, allow myself to go that far?"[91] Her father, when sought out for his advice, tells her no. "You must be the one to hold back. Don't go upstairs so often, don't encourage him more than you can help," he says. "It is the man who is always the active one in these things: the woman can hold him back." When Anne defends Peter as a "nice boy," her father counters that he is "not a strong character." Linking sexual desire, or its control, to character, Anne's father tells her in no uncertain terms—as plenty of parents in 1944 did and plenty of parents today continue to do—that good girls resist. And in so doing, help good boys remain that way.

But Anne rejects her father's advice, continuing to go upstairs alone to visit Peter, asserting, "I want to be able to go on in my own way too, the way I think is right."[92] Then, after having slipped a letter into her father's pocket essentially reiterating her stance, she is devastated. Her father has chastised her severely, and she has lost all faith in herself. How could she possibly have assumed that her ideas were just and right? "My pride has been shaken a bit, for I was becoming much too taken up with myself again," she says. "What Miss Anne does is by no means always right!" By challenging her parents' judgment, she has hurt their feelings. "I ought to be deeply ashamed of myself, and indeed I am," she says.[93]

After this, her relationship with Peter changes. She closes off her "inner self" from him, insisting, "If he wants to force the lock again he'll have to work a good deal harder than before."[94]

As Anne questions her world, she also wavers; her views are at odds with those of so many. The doubt she begins to feel about herself and her convictions — especially given the historical context of her writing, a time in which so many people acted utterly without conscience — is heartbreaking. "I wonder if it's really a good quality not to let myself be influenced," she writes on July 6, 1944. "Is it really good to follow almost entirely my own conscience?"[95] A week later, she writes, "This 'self-consciousness' haunts me, and every time I open my mouth I know as soon as I've spoken whether 'that ought to have been different' or 'that was right as it was.' There are so many things about myself that I condemn; I couldn't begin to name them all."[96]

In this same entry, she writes, "Daddy tried all he could to check my rebellious spirit, but it was no use, I have cured myself, by seeing for myself what was wrong in my behavior and keeping it before my eyes." But she vehemently resists her father's efforts to dismiss her feelings as a stage she is going through. Her feelings are genuine, her convictions deeply felt. "I didn't want to hear about 'symptoms of your age,' or 'it wears off by itself'; I didn't want to be treated as a girl-like-all-others, but as Anne-on-her-own-merits." The effect? "These things have made me never mention my views on life nor my well-considered theories to anyone but my diary and, occasionally, to [my sister] Margot."

In Anne's very last diary entry, three days before the Annexe is raided and its inhabitants arrested, Anne describes herself as having developed a "dual personality." She says, "I never utter my real feelings about anything." She acts cheerful and superficial because she is afraid that if she lets her finer, serious and thoughtful, side show, people will laugh at her. "I know exactly how I'd like to be, how I am too . . . inside," she writes. "But, alas, I'm only like that for myself." The very last sentence of her very last diary entry reads thus:

> Finally I twist my heart round again, so that the bad is on the outside and the good is on the inside and keep on trying to find a way of becoming what I would so like to be, and what I could be, if . . . there weren't any other people living in the world.[97]

It's dramatic stuff. The hyperbole and the sentiments she expresses seem exaggerated and occasionally self-aggrandizing. But for teenage Anne Frank, these inner battles generated nearly the same intensity of feelings as the battles that raged in the world outside her Annexe window. Had Anne survived World War II and published her diary the way she intended, she probably would have returned to this manuscript with the "objectivity" of an adult, and her inner struggles, if they survived her editing, would have manifested themselves with the amusingly ironic touch of an adult author. But Anne's war, which "reigns incessantly within"—this meticulous ferreting out and recording of the conflicting forces at work to shape her person—remains in its rawest state. Anne is a cocky, confident, opinionated girl. But she is brutally aware of others' efforts to reconfigure, or dilute, her personality. The passages of her diary speak to her inner battle; at stake is her sense of self.

To return to authors Carol Gilligan, Peggy Orenstein, and Mary Pipher, who have argued that girls start losing their confidence and their sense of self when they are Anne's age, it is interesting to read Anne's diary as a record of that transformation. Anne loses confidence in the power of her ideas, and shortly thereafter, in herself. Her changing body is first a delight and then a battleground. Desire competes with custom, and the right to conduct a romantic encounter as she sees fit is curtailed by her father, who reminds her that it is her job to *resist* sexual exploration. The elaborate etiquette surrounding menstruation, sexuality, and desire defies reason; when the rules first fail to make sense, Anne dismisses them; when they continue to do so, she dismisses herself.

PART THREE

The Adult: PMS,

the Scourge of the Nineties

When Molly and Judy Blume's Margaret grow up, their enthusiasm for womanhood undoubtedly wanes. In fact, the confused reluctance of girls like Anne Frank—or D.J. and myself—turns out to be warranted. Womanhood *is* a dubious honor, and the hormones that bring on menstruation are once again to blame. As teens we resisted the grown-ups who dismissed our complaints—or our blue Mead memo manifestos—as "just a stage," only to discover as adults that our concerns are often similarly trivialized, this time as PMS—premenstrual syndrome.

Originally confined to medical texts, PMS has slipped so comfortably into our cultural lexicon today that it explains away a colleague's crankiness, a couple's marital strife, or a mother's short-tempered treatment of her kids. We use it to dismiss the testy comments of a friend—"She's PMS-ing"—or our own grouchiness—"Sorry, PMS." If we're depressed or sad, using PMS as an explanation can have an almost magnetic appeal. And it's good for a laugh, frequent fodder for the humor mill.

More troubling, though, is the way in which the term has become a convenient catchall for women's complaints, a way of discounting women's anger—and their often legitimate concerns—by attributing their dissatisfaction to hormones. (Conversely, it provides an acceptable excuse for women who are reluctant to claim their anger: "I was not myself.") Because a woman's anger or depression affects others—husbands, colleagues, family—society has been quick to embrace PMS as an explanation for it. And anxious to cure it.

But while conventional wisdom holds women's hormones responsible for one weepy week per month, the experts are not so sure. In fact, reputable doctors and scientists continue to argue about every single aspect of PMS. They debate whether or not PMS is serious enough to qualify as a "disorder"; whether the cure for it is drug therapy; whether labeling it as an illness is beneficial for women personally, politically, or culturally; and even whether PMS-induced mood swings exist at all. With so many conflicting studies being generated, it's important to put the research into context: to ask who benefits from the cures, who defines "abnormal" anger or sadness, how self-diagnosis might skew research results, and how self-fulfilling a prophecy PMS can be. Today, women are bombarded with headlines, anecdotes, and studies implying that extreme mood swings are an inevitable part of our menstrual cycle. But how do we separate cultural expectations from biological givens? The two strands are intertwined in alarming ways.

According to the media—which cites psychologists, scientists, social workers, doctors, and professors in more than seven hundred articles during the past two years alone—America is a nation of cranky women. The American College of Obstetricians and Gynecologists puts the figure of PMS sufferers at 40 percent of all American women, with 8 percent of all women debilitated by the disease. Other estimates, especially those of self-help-book authors, say that 70 percent of all American women suffer from PMS. Still others put the figure even higher, at 90 percent—especially when spouses and boyfriends are tallied among the victims. (And they should be, insists Dr. Katharina Dalton, who coined the term *PMS* in 1954. "PMS is a man's problem too," she reminds us in her seminal book *Once a Month.* "With about 40% of women suffering from PMS, the law of averages ensures that sooner or later a man will find himself on the receiving end."[1]).

While collecting victims, PMS has also gobbled up almost half a menstruating woman's days. Once upon a time, PMS was confined to the week before menstruation. Now its eminently mutable definition has oozed out over the edges of that week right into the next, as a euphemism for bleeding itself. (One woman in a 1997 menstrual products focus group said she never used the word *menstruation* with her friends: "I just say I'm PMS-ing, and pretty much everybody knows that means I'm having my period.")

Perhaps most telling—and a signal that PMS has swept past the medical profession and consequently into our culture at large—is the disorder's appearance in the 1994 edition of the *Diagnostic and Statistical Manual,* the mental health professional's bible. Here the illness is given the formal name of premenstrual dysphoric disorder. Psychiatrists translate this into lay terms as "extreme moodiness."

Despite the fact that no single reputable scientific experiment has isolated fluctuating hormones as the cause of PMS, almost every expert in the field attributes the "disease" to them. And if it's physical, the reasoning goes, then we can fix it. (And make money doing so.) To that end, hundreds of cures have been floated.

The federal government, public and private universities, charitable and research foundations, and drug companies have all jumped on the PMS bandwagon. In their quest for a cure, they have conducted treatment studies on the following: magnesium; zinc; oil of evening primrose; salt; light, natural and artificial; progesterone, natural and synthetic, given orally, anally, and by injection; Prozac, Paxil, and Zoloft, administered daily or "as needed"; carbohydrates and carbohydrate beverages, such as PMS Escape; fatty acids; gonadotropin-releasing hormone; mefenamic acid, an anti-inflammatory; thyroid pills; tranquilizers; vitamin E; vitamin B_6; vitamin C; multiple vitamin supplements; the antibiotic doxycycline; lithium; exercise; birth-control pills; diuretics; tea; and even hysterectomies.

Academic and medical journals are littered with articles analyzing symptoms, exploring promising cures, and ruling out causes. Studies run the gamut, with titles like "Randomized Controlled Study of Premenstrual Symptoms Treated with Ear, Hand, and Foot Reflexology" (published in *Obstetrics and Gynecology* in 1993) and "Changes in Premenstrual Symptoms and Irrational Thinking Following Cognitive-Behavioral Coping Skills Training" (appearing in the *Journal of Consulting Clinical Psychology* in 1994).[2]

Because there is little consensus about what causes or cures PMS—and it is the mood swings, not the physical discomforts associated with the ensuing cramps or headaches, that get the attention—there is room for everyone in this field, no matter how untried. "Experts" get around uneven results by saying the treatment is complicated and needs to be tailored to the individual. To that end, more than 115 PMS clinics or treatment centers have sprung up across the country, many of them af-filiated with prestigious universities like Columbia and the University of Pennsylvania. And hundreds of thousands more women are being encouraged to self-diagnose.[3] Instructions for self-diagnosis have appeared in dozens of books published on the topic, including Dalton's *Once a Month*, Martorano and Morgan's *Unmasking PMS*, and Bender's *PMS: Women Tell Women How to Control Premenstrual Syndrome*.[4] This does not include cameo appearances of PMS in books on other subjects, such as Gillian Ford's *What's Wrong with My Hormones?*[5]

Using PMS as a tidy physical explanation can have an al-most magnetic appeal to women who characterize themselves as "angry" and "out of control." "It's a tremendous relief for women to find out that what they're suffering from has a name," Jean Endicott, a clinical psychologist and director of the Premenstrual Evaluation Unit at Columbia-Presbyterian Medical Center, told *Ms.* magazine in July 1996.[6] Today Endi-cott celebrates PMS's flight from obscurity to fame. "This is a condition worthy of recognition," she says. "And, because of studies that are published in journals that are highly respected, I do think the medical profession is more aware of it now. That makes a very big difference when a woman walks into a doc-tor's office." She recalls the days when women with PMS were dismissed as crazy. "Now there are treatments," she says, refer-ring to a recent discovery that women suffering from PMS fared better on Prozac.

And indeed, more and more women are being treated for what was once considered a rare illness. After all, PMS has stock-piled symptoms at an alarming rate. More than 150 sometimes contradictory symptoms, such as insomnia and hypersomnia, have accrued since the fifteen first identified in the 1950s — and they seem to have swallowed up an entire gender. Most Americans now believe *all* women suffer from some form of PMS.

IN THE BEGINNING THERE WAS PREMENSTRUAL TENSION: DR. DALTON IDENTIFIES AN ILLNESS, CARVES A NICHE, AND REAPS A PROFIT

PMS is a notorious illness. Revisionists suggest that it's been around for eons, citing Simonides of Ceos' poem about the changing moods of women (written about 500 B.C.), Queen Victoria's nastiness, and Lizzie Borden's murderous rage as proof positive. But it wasn't until 1953 that Britain's Dr. Katharina Dalton first itemized a set of symptoms and labeled them PMS. In the forty years since, the acronym has mutated into shorthand for "irrational anger." Or rather, an irrationally angry woman.

We have Dr. Dalton, a PMS guru who campaigns tirelessly on behalf of this illness, to thank for that. She founded the world's first PMS clinic, and today boasts that she has successfully treated more than fifty thousand women. Wildly controversial at the time, four decades later her criteria for categorizing PMS are nearly universally embraced by the medical establishment. While there is no medical test for PMS — indeed, no physical cause for it has ever been discovered — Dalton's self-diagnosing menstrual chart has evolved into the industry standard. Her work spawned the most common PMS treatment out there: megadoses of the hormone progesterone. As one of the leading authorities on PMS, she has published repeatedly in the *British Medical Journal*, the *British Journal of Family Planning*, and the *Journal of the American Medical Association*. In the past decade alone she has published more than twenty-eight journal articles and four books on PMS. Her PMS handbook, *Once a Month*, was first published in 1978 and is now in its fifth printing. In it she explains why the high cost of PMS, "measured in millions of pounds, liras, kroners [*sic*], and dollars, as well as in terms of human misery, unhappiness, and pain," threatens the very foundations of our society.[7]

If unchecked, PMS can be responsible for shoddy workmanship, criminal activity, marital breakdowns, and distracted, even dangerous, mothering, she says, warning her readers: "These are not trivialities, but are matters of vital concern to the patient, her family, society, and maybe even the nation."[8]

When I interviewed Dr. Dalton by telephone, she spoke with all the weight of her impressive body of research behind her, growing positively churlish at the mention of critics who doubted her progesterone cure. "That's just plain stupid," she said dismissively when I mentioned that some researchers had called her methodology flawed. She is as grandiose in person as she is hyperbolic in her work. (*Once a Month* reads as if hordes of angry women are ripping at our social fabric with bared teeth.)

Dalton, who frequently neglects to cite sources for her figures, claims that "[PMS] has been estimated to cost U.S. industry 8% of its total wage bill." Explaining that during the paramenstruum, the period encompassing the week before menstruation and the week of menstruation, "there is a deterioration of arm and hand steadiness," she warns that "the industries that suffer most are those employing large numbers of women." Referring to a clumsy, PMS-ing podiatrist who confided to her, "If I ever cut a patient, I'm sure it will be during those premenstrual days," Dalton goes on to wonder "if the same ever applies to surgeons." Accidents at work and lowered mental ability are also problems. "More than one secretary has been referred for treatment when her boss could no longer put up with those few days every month when letters had to be repeatedly returned for retyping."[9] And certain jobs have their own particular hazards. She describes a "hoarseness that affects opera and other professional singers," "a lowered sensitivity to taste [that] is a handicap to cooks who may overflavor the sauces," and PMS-induced "bad-tempered service by salespeople, receptionists, and waitresses." One contrite teacher even wrote Dalton a letter confessing, "Every month there are one or two days when I am simply not worth the salary my employers pay me." Dalton's solution? "Women can be assigned to less-skilled jobs such as packing and stacking during their vulnerable days, rather than remaining on tasks that are much more complex and harder to correct later."[10]

But, Dalton warns, the solution is not to send women home, since ladies of leisure face their own set of hazards. "Even when a woman is away from the office and the housework and just relaxing, the black cloud of once-a-month problems may still be with her." She advises against playing tennis, golf, or racquetball, since "arm and hand steadiness is impaired, sharpness of vision declines, and movement is slower because of extra weight and water retention." Hobbies also pose problems. "There are those who enjoy dressmaking, but know better than to cut a dress out of expensive material on the wrong day of the month in case they spoil it. Others hesitate to buy flowers at that time, as they find they cannot arrange them to their satisfaction." Even driving to your job or recreational activity is problematic. Not just for PMS-ing drivers, who are prone to accidents, but even for their PMS-ing passengers. "In the few seconds between a car climbing a curb and before it hits a wall an alert passenger may brace herself and cover her head for protection, but the passenger in her paramenstruum may be too slow to take even these elementary precautions," Dalton reports. Forego even the most mundane pleasures during PMS, she suggests. Shopping, for example, isn't safe: "A woman may become an indecisive, hesitant shopper who tries on all the shoes in the shop, finds they won't fit her swollen feet, and leaves empty-handed." Worse still, "she may buy totally inappropriate dresses that don't fit and are the wrong color, and which she will never wear. It is possible that her color sense and appreciation of shape and size deteriorate during this phase of the cycle."[11]

Sadly, the victim's family bears the brunt of the PMS burden. It is easy to spot a PMS-ing mother, Dalton writes, because "the usually tidy house is not picked up, the beds aren't made, dirty dishes sit on the kitchen table, and there is probably a burned cake by the sink. Perhaps the children went off to school late, in yesterday's clothes, and chances are that meals will not be ready on time."[12] Citing this letter as an example of the recurring themes she heard from women—"Since the birth of my last child 2 years ago (I have five children), I have changed from being a normal housewife and mother to an unpredictable, bad-tempered person"—Dalton places the blame for dissatisfaction in women squarely on their hormones.[13]

These hormones have the potential to make women both unpleasant wives and unfit mothers. "If the mother is accident-
prone during her paramenstruum, the children in her care are
also accident-prone," Dalton explains. "And if she is tired during the paramenstruum, she may not notice little Johnny running toward an oncoming car or climbing a dangerous tree,
and so he will be in even greater danger then." As proof of this,
Dalton cites a 1970 survey of children who were admitted as
emergencies to the North Middlesex Hospital in London: 49
percent of the mothers were in their paramenstruum on the
day the child was admitted.[14] But if the paramenstruum is defined as the week before your period plus the week of your
period—in other words, two weeks out of every month—
wouldn't it make sense that 50 percent of all women would
have to be in their paramenstruum at any given time, whether
in the emergency room or on the street? And weren't some of
the kids in the emergency room ill, as opposed to being accident victims? Dalton dismisses my skepticism, saying I've
missed the point. A mother's PMS can precipitate illnesses
such as asthma, in their children, she asserts.

While Dalton's discoveries may call into question the com-
petence of most of the world's moms, the consequences for
motherhood are hardly dire. After all, few replacements are
itching to enter this unglamorous, unpaid profession. Where
Dalton's argument gets downright spooky is when she turns
her sight on professional women. "The problems of lowered
judgment during the premenstruum must be considered by
teachers, judges, and executives, who need to be on their
guard against making hasty and wrong decisions," she warns.[15]
But when asked whether her book reinforces stereotypes of

women as unreliable workers, Dalton is dismissive. "Oh God, no, they're not unfit workers," she says, refusing to see how her work might be interpreted that way. Instead, she launches into a diatribe about PMS criminals: "Premenstrually there are those women who commit crime. But women commit far less crimes than men, you see, because they're only committing crimes during that one week a month. Not all month long like men." She then offers this peculiar reasoning for why employers should still hire women. "Women are far more reliable workers [than men] because alcohol is such a problem with men. The high level of alcoholism among men makes a high absentee rate for them. Men have absenteeism all the time, women have it in bouts, only when they're PMS." (In fact, a 1985 study by the U.S. Department of Labor found that women, on average, missed one more day of work a year than men. But instead of tying this to PMS, the study noted that the higher absentee rate was occurring among women in their childbearing years—suggesting that Mom, not Dad, was the one going to Junior's parent-teacher conference, taking him to the dentist, or staying home with him when he was sick.) But Dalton thinks it's silly to worry about the way PMS might be used against women. "I think that's dumb. That's coming from people who haven't really thought through this issue."

A CYCLICAL HISTORY

Studies of women's menstrual cycles have an interesting way of being recycled at politically expedient points in history. It seems every time women start demanding access to this or that, there is a rash of studies "proving" women's menstrual cycles render them unsuitable for . . . whatever.

In 1878, when doctors were faced with the question of whether to admit women to medical schools, the *British Medical Journal* published a discussion about whether menstruating women spoiled meat when they touched it. Checking in on the debate, one doctor, anticipating Dalton by one hundred years, wrote, "If such bad results accrue from a woman curing dead meat whilst she is menstruating, what would result, under similar conditions, from her attempt to cure living flesh in her midwifery or surgical practice?"

The answer to his question was a flurry of studies asserting that women's cycling constitutions rendered them unfit for sustained mental labor, as well as for physical labor. These studies coincided with a larger debate going on in the United States during the late 1870s and the 1880s. At the time, Americans were hotly disputing the question of higher education for women, and menstruation figured prominently in their arguments against it. Henry Maudsley, writing in his oft-quoted *Sex in Mind and Education* (1883), epitomized popular opinion—dressed up as "scientific truth"—when he observed that girls were doomed to failure in college because of menstruation. He insisted:

This is a matter of physiology, not a matter of sentiment; it is not a mere question of larger or smaller muscles, but of the energy and power of endurance, of the nerve force which drives the intellectual and muscular machinery; not a question of two bodies and minds that are in equal physical condition, but of one body and mind capable of sustained and regular hard labor, and of another body and mind which for one quarter of each month, during the best years of life, is more or less sick and unfit for hard work.[16]

Maudsley's definition of "hard work," of course, was sporadically applied: no one was worrying that the fragile cook, servant girl, or farmer's wife was being overly taxed at "that time of month." And when women pressed ahead, attended college, and excelled in the halls of learning, the debate about menstrual cycles shifted from women's suitability for higher education to their suitability for public life in general. When the pesky suffragettes were asking to participate in the political process, experts were retaliating with more "scientific" studies proving that women belonged in the domestic sphere; menstruation figured prominently among the reasons. Women's fickle hormones simply weren't to be trusted.

At the turn of the century, an entire "psychology of the ovary" developed. In their 1978 book *For Her Own Good*, Barbara Ehrenreich and Deirdre English describe a nineteenth-century catchall illness that, like PMS, was held to be responsible for a host of problems. "Since the ovaries controlled the personality, they must be responsible for any psychological disorders: conversely, psychological disorders were a sure sign of ovarian disease. Ergo, the organs must be removed." These "ovariotomies" seemed to play the same role that hysterectomies play with modern women. Noting that patients were often brought in by their husbands, Ehrenreich and English quote an 1893 advocate of the operation who claimed that "patients are improved, some of them cured; . . . the moral sense of the patient is elevated . . . she becomes tractable, orderly, industrious, and cleanly."[17]

Doctors were announcing this new syndrome just as women were beginning to timidly request a bit more power in the political process and to express some dissatisfaction with their carefully circumscribed roles. And the invalids weren't viewed as aberrations, but rather as examples of some intrinsic female weakness. Because the disease sprang from women's reproductive organs, people began to believe that all women suffered from it, on some level. "[The disease] had become so widespread as to represent not so much a disease in the medical sense as a way of life," Ehrenreich and English explained. "More precisely, the way this type of woman was expected to live predisposed her to sickness, and sickness in turn predisposed her to continue to live as she was expected to." Naturally, stress was determined to be the cause of this epidemic, and the most famous treatment was Dr. S. Weir Mitchell's rest cure. Sufferers were ordered to withdraw from everything— not to tax their brains or bodies—and lie in bed, in a dark room, doing nothing. Women were at the mercy of their reproductive cycles, and this made them weak, volatile, and (ideally) housebound. Scientists and doctors cranked out reports on woman's fragility, and shrill reports in the media generated a debate that quickly reached a feverish pitch. Leta Stetter Hollingworth, Ph.D., whose 1914 book *Functional Periodicity: An Experimental Study of the Mental and Motor Abilities of Women During Menstruation* debunked many of the myths out there, described the hysteria this way:

Men to whom it would never have occurred to write authoritatively on any other subject regarding which they possessed no reliable or expert knowledge, have not hesitated to make the most positive statements regarding the mental and motor abilities of women as related to functional periodicity . . . It is positively asserted that women cannot successfully pursue professional and industrial life because they are incapacitated, and should rest for one-fifth of their time.[18]

As Hollingworth observes, there is nothing subtle about using these menstrual studies as a means of barring women from public life—when convenient. *The New York Times* made the connection explicit in an article published on March 28, 1912:

No doctor can ever lose sight of the fact that the mind of a woman is always threatened with danger from the reverberations of her physiological emergencies [menstruation]. It is with such thoughts that the doctor lets his eyes rest upon the militant suffragist. He cannot shut them to the fact that there is mixed up in the woman's movement such mental disorder, and he cannot conceal from himself the physiological emergencies which lie behind.

In 1914 a skeptical Hollingworth decided to conduct a study of her own. Reasoning that if the nervous system were truly in a state of agitation, we would indeed see some kind of physical effect from it, she took twenty-three women and gave them a battery of tests, for an hour every day over several months, after they had eaten dinner. Among the tests she had them do were a tapping test (to see how many times they could tap a board in a set time), a steadiness test (where they had to hold a pole in a round hole without letting it touch the sides), and a typing test (where speed, accuracy, and concentration could be measured). She discovered . . . nothing. There was no discernible pattern in the women's efficiency levels. "The variability of performance is not affected by physiological periodicity," she concluded. "It is difficult to understand such striking disparity between what has been accepted and the figures yielded by scientific method." She suggested that the "mystery" and "caprice" of popular culture had permeated this arena of scientific inquiry. "The dogma once formulated, has been quoted on authority from author to author until the present day."[19]

Once women won the right to vote in 1920, the menstruation-equals-inadequacy debate simmered down for a while. In fact, two decades later, new "proof" arrived that women were perfectly fit and capable—even when bleeding—and therefore should step right up and join the war effort. When Rosie the Riveter was needed in U.S. factories, the Women's Army Corps began scouring the kitchens of America for recruits. "I want a women's corps right away, and I don't want any excuses," General Marshall announced in the aftermath of Pearl Harbor. During World War II, menstrual limitations were dismissed as nonsense. In fact, studies and commentary went in the other direction, extolling the virtues of women workers and soldiers. When the first batch of WACs were put to work, an army report gleefully stated: "They are superior to men in all functions involving delicacy or manual dexterity, such as operation at the director, height finder, radar, and searchlight control systems. They perform routine repetitious tasks in a manner superior to men."[20] (This was a far cry from Representative Newt Gingrich's 1995 declaration that women shouldn't be anywhere near combat because "females have biological problems staying in a ditch for 30 days because they get infections.") And if any of Uncle Sam's soldiers were tempted to make it relevant—or use the old excuse of cramps—instructional films were produced to persuade them otherwise.

An official training film put out by the War Department in the 1940s, called *Strictly Personal*, coached novice WACs on nutrition, rest, and exercise, reminding them to keep active and fit for duty. When one of the women soldiers lies listlessly on her cot—"I can't drill today, I feel unwell," she whines—a fellow soldier tells her to buck up and take a shower. A voice-over reinforces this advice by introducing us to an expert, "the Doctor," who reiterates the absurdity of the woman's complaint. "Some twentieth-century girls still believe that lavender-and-old-lace hokum about no activity and no bathing during menstruation," the Doctor tells us. "That's Victorian stuff. And so is that trash about nerves and sensibility during this period." As we watch a scene in which a Victorian woman in a lavish four-poster bed throws a tantrum at the serving girl bringing her breakfast, a voice-over by the Doctor informs us, "Women are where they are today because they have learned to take it in stride." The Doctor continues: "But when I tell some of the women that menstruation is no excuse for absenteeism and self-coddling, they look quite hurt and bewildered and start bombarding me with questions." With military precision, a line of women marches toward the camera as the women fire off questions: "Do the nerves always go to pieces?" "Are we expected to suffer and just go about our business?" "What if you have the cramps and have to go to bed?" A military medical officer interrupts the questions with a quick anatomy lesson and her cure for cramps. "If your posture is good and your abdominal muscles firm, you'll suffer less pain during menstruation." After a quick detour into a discussion of douches and sanitary protection—"The choice between the external pad and tampon is a purely personal one" and "The tampon fits into the vagina like this . . ."—the film ends. Women learn that these hygienic tips are all they need "to do the man-sized job you've enlisted for."

After the end of World War II, when the supplemental women's army was looking to downsize and male soldiers were returning to their jobs, Rosie the Riveter was sent home with a rash of new studies "proving" that children needed their moms at home, that the workplace was potentially hazardous to women's unborn children, and that women's cycles made them less-competent workers than men. Enter Dr. Katharina Dalton, circa 1950, with a name for this sweeping and debilitating affliction: premenstrual syndrome.

Historically, women's hormones—or, before those hormones were identified, women's uteruses or menstrual cycles—have been blamed for consumption, insanity, dyspepsia, nervous prostration, rheumatism, hysteria, headaches, muscular aches, weakness, depression, indigestion, paleness, troublesomeness, "eating like a ploughman," masturbation, attempted suicide, erotic tendencies, persecution mania, and "simple 'cussedness.'" Later, when PMS entered the popular lexicon, women's hormones became responsible for marital strife; poor job performance; depression, anxiety, and tension; feelings of hopelessness, sadness, anger, and irritability; interpersonal conflicts; decreased interest in work, school, friends, and hobbies; difficulty in concentrating; overeating; hypersomnia and insomnia;

breast tenderness; joint or muscle pain; bloating; achiness; acne; aggressiveness; constipation and diarrhea; dizziness; edema; fatigue; food cravings; forgetfulness; headaches; hot flashes; mood swings; nausea; palpitations; restlessness and lethargy; tearfulness; tension; weight gain; social withdrawal; asthma; child abuse; car accidents; shoplifting; and even murder (Dalton has testified on behalf of several female defendants, claiming that severe PMS drove them to violence).[21]

THE PROGESTERONE CURE

There *is* hope for PMS sufferers. "Relief from PMS is here, in your hands," Dr. Katharina Dalton promises on the jacket of her book. Her cure? Progesterone supplements. And carbohydrates.

For more than thirty years, Dalton has been treating women with the steroid hormone progesterone — via vaginal suppositories, anal suppositories, and occasionally injection. Despite conflicting studies about the efficacy of these hormone supplements, she cites anecdotal evidence as proof and claims a remarkable success rate — fifty thousand women cured! Even her discovery of the progesterone treatment was based on personal experience, she confided to me in an interview. She had had migraines that retreated during her pregnancy, and her gynecologist, mentioning the mega-amounts of progesterone women produce during the last two trimesters, prescribed the steroid for her headaches. Dalton's migraines disappeared. Dalton took this information and ran with it, dispensing progesterone to all her PMS patients and broadcasting the positive results. "When a woman with PMS who has been treated with progesterone returns to the doctor, it is often difficult to recognize her as the same person," Dalton declared. Best of all: "There is the husband who comes in to tell you about his wife who is 'now like the woman I married.'"[22]

Despite the fact that Dalton's study depended on patients subjectively self-diagnosing themselves as PMS sufferers (and self-reporting the results), offered no control group for contrast, and presented no evidence that these women actually lacked progesterone in their systems, gynecologists and general practitioners across Europe and the United States dove in, prescribing progesterone to women in huge doses. Nearly half a century later, scientists remain unable to document any progesterone deficiency among PMS sufferers and have discovered that placebos have an identical efficacy rate. Still, Dalton and the American PMS clinics her work has spawned push the steroid like candy.

In the United States, the primary source for information about PMS is Women's Health America Group, a for-profit company in Wisconsin. Marla Ahlgrimm, founder and president, says it has gathered plenty of anecdotal evidence that progesterone works. "In our experience, the best way to approach managing PMS is by incorporating a number of things," says Ahlgrimm, explaining that her group recommends dietary changes and exercise first. "Certain nutritional supplements are also helpful; then a prescription of progesterone would be the next step." Over three thousand women a month call the company's PMS hot line, an 800 number that connects them with pharmacists who talk them through their symptoms. Many of the callers are helped by the progesterone this phone-order pharmacy promises to mix up individually and mail out the next day.

Known colloquially as PMS Access, Ahlgrimm's group sounds like any of the dozens of nonprofits that dispense disease information, such as the American Cancer Society or the American Heart Association, but it's not. While most of the callers contact PMS Access for the same reasons people call the Lupus Foundation of America—they wonder if they have the disease or what the latest treatments are—the response they get is slightly different. At PMS Access, those who wonder whether they fall into the PMS camp are treated to a brochure titled "The Odds Are Almost Even." Declared PMS-ers get free advice about exercise and dietary changes. Then they get a catalog of PMS books and videos—for sale. Then PMS Access tells them about a vitamin-and-mineral supplement called Procycle—which it sells. And, if that doesn't work, PMS Access tells them about natural progesterone—which it also sells; just have your doctor call in a prescription. "Since some doctors aren't as educated about progesterone as they should be, we also have a manual about it that we'll send to them," explains PMS Access spokesperson Debra Short. "Or doctors can call and talk directly to one of our pharmacists." PMS Access senior pharmacist Scott Stampfer sings the praises of progesterone and offers anecdotal "proof" of its efficacy. "I don't think we'd be here if the medication were some kind of placebo," he tells me.

Stephanie DeGraff Bender, co-author of *PMS: Women Tell Women How to Control Premenstrual Syndrome* and director of the Full Circle Women's Health Clinic in Boulder, Colorado, says her group also steers women toward changes in diet and exercise before talking about progesterone. But they're awfully glad the option exists. "It's controversial, and yet in the seventeen years I've been working in this field I've yet to see anything that works better," says Bender.

Anecdotal evidence is one thing. But while Dalton and her minions go about merrily dispensing progesterone, a persuasive body of scientific studies is discrediting the remedy. According to *Psychiatric Annals*, which dedicated its September 1996 issue to PMS, progesterone has been the most studied of all hormonal treatments for this disorder.[23] Recently, eight double-blind studies (meaning that neither the subjects nor the experimenters know which subjects are taking hormones and which are taking sugar pills) have shown progesterone to be no more effective than the placebos. In 1995 Ellen Freeman, the research director for the University of Pennsylvania's PMS program, and her colleagues published a study in the *Journal of the American Medical Association* suggesting that progesterone was simply a profitable hoax.[24] While she doesn't dispute the fact that Dalton, Bender, and the folks at PMS Access have had some success with progesterone, she does point to controlled clinical trials as proof that something else beside progesterone might be at work. Otherwise, a double-blind study would back up the treatment. "That's the purpose of doing this kind of study," Freeman says, defending her work. "This happens to be the gold standard of drug studies in the United States." Still, she admits that some women probably did get better on progesterone. "People get better for many different reasons," she says. "They get better because they feel supported by clinicians, because they feel understood, because their symptoms may naturally wax and wane over time, and, more importantly, women may show some improvement because they feel much more control over what's going on and can manage their symptoms better as a result."

But Dalton holds fast to her progesterone cure. "Freeman did a ridiculous trial," she says, insisting that her results were skewed because she used minute amounts of progesterone instead of megadoses. "And unless you keep an eye on the food you're consuming, you can't get any progesterone absorbed." However, today Dalton tailors her explanation somewhat, admitting that it's probably not inadequate progesterone in the blood but inadequate progesterone receptors at the cell level that are responsible for PMS. "Of course, I haven't seen any papers—aside from mine—that look at that!" she says indignantly.

PMS SPEAKOUT: DEFINING A PROBLEM

In its 1992 edition, that bible of the women's health movement, *Our Bodies, Ourselves*, took on the topic of PMS. Here the authors, all medical professionals well versed in feminist debate, not only speculated about the pros and cons of progesterone but took the critique one step further, observing that "the placebo response rate is so high for PMS that uncontrolled trials make all remedies seem effective." They went on to affirm what many doctors and the PMS industry—PMS clinics, PMS researchers, and PMS pharmacies—deny: "The number and severity of the symptoms alone do not distinguish those who report having PMS from those who don't report it." What did distinguish the two groups was this: "The women with PMS had lower self-esteem, were more likely to blame themselves for negative events, felt guiltier over being angry, avoided stressful events, were more likely to wish problems would go away rather than attempt to solve them, kept their feelings to themselves and felt more stress." In conclusion, the writers were circumspect: "This sounds pretty close to the prescription for being a good female."*[25]

Indeed, the limited statistics that exist on PMS sufferers are beginning to bear this out. These women are typically in their mid-thirties (peak child-rearing and career-advancement years), typically have several children, and typically work outside the home. Stephanie DeGraff Bender, co-author of the PMS self-help book *PMS: Women Tell Women How to Control Premenstrual Syndrome*, reports that 42 percent of the women visiting her Full Circle Women's Health Clinic for PMS are either currently divorced or have been divorced in the past, which means a sizable number are single moms. The women typically report feeling "overwhelmed," and are nearly all frightened by the uncontrollable anger that has them lashing out

---

*Interestingly, the language is toned down a bit in the 1998 version of the book. According to Nancy Reame, who co-authored the chapter on menstruation, Reame and her colleagues worried that "maybe this was blaming the victim too much." They were also concerned that the earlier edition made their conclusions sound definitive when research into the link between PMS and "life stressors" was still inconclusive. In this new edition, they remind women that "the term 'PMS' may encourage us to relate to more and more of our premenstrual experiences as medical problems" and suggest that "[if we] feel more comfortable with our moods as well as our anger, we may experience many of our premenstrual signs differently." The new *Our Bodies, Ourselves* also warns women of the dangers of overprescribing. "Many of the treatments prescribed for 'PMS' are expensive (progesterone, fluoxetine) and can have serious side effects when taken in large doses over long periods of time (vitamin B_6, fluoxetine)" (p. 281).

against their children, colleagues, and, in particular, spouses. All of the self-help books have a section on helping spouses cope. (Bender's book quotes Mark, a 45-year-old psychiatrist whose wife is "wonderful" most of the time: "Then there are those times when, excuse me, she is a real bitch. She's argumentative, overly emotional, sarcastic, and the last person I want to be around."[26]) Dalton even suggests that husbands be the ones to identify the disease and insist that their wives get help. "Frequently, it is the man in her life who first makes the connection and recognizes a woman's menstrual cyclicity," Dalton writes. She says a man may awake one morning to "a hysterical and completely irrational woman," one who is "pessimistic, negative, and withdrawn at times, and nothing can be done to please her. She may be snappy, argumentative, impatient, and illogical; or she may shout, shriek, yell, and swear." Dalton suggests that husbands simply ignore their wives' complaints. "It is also no use arguing logically during the premenstruum; just wait until the postmenstruum when she will be calmer and ready to listen — although she may then be tormented with guilt at her earlier behavior." Dalton suggests that husbands make appointments for their wives to get treated and "tell the doctor how it is affecting your life as well as hers."[27]

But Dr. Anne Walker, who has studied PMS, takes issue with that. Critiquing studies that exaggerate both the size and nature of the problem, she says, "[PMS] has been blown up out of all proportion." In a 1993 article in *The Guardian*, Walker elaborated on this: "If you walk down the street and you look at all these women, you think, well, statistically 25 percent of them are premenstrual, and the world carries on." While she admits that most women would recognize symptoms from the premenstrual repertoire— irritability, fatigue —she questions whether they constitute a disease, even though the women's partners might insist the symptoms are a problem. She wonders who is being put upon here, suggesting, "We should be worrying about who wants to call it an illness and who's being inconvenienced."[28]

When one studies the examples cited in scientific journals, self-help books, and magazine articles, a troubling pattern emerges. And given the anecdotal nature of the "proof" that PMS is the problem, it's easy to review these same stories but draw different conclusions. For example, in their book *PMS: Women Tell Women How to Control Premenstrual Syndrome*, Stephanie DeGraff Bender and Kathleen Kelleher provide several illuminating examples of patients describing their problems. One segment, called "Nancy's Story," reads this way:

Let's say I have errands to run. I ask my family: "Please have the kitchen cleaned before I get back."

It sounds reasonable enough. But when I get back, the dishes aren't done, and everyone's watching TV. No one bothers to offer an excuse. The scene is set for World War III to start.

"I can't believe the dishes aren't done!" I say.

Then my voice goes up a couple of notches. "I can't believe that you're all just sitting around watching TV. No one ever does anything they say they're going to do! I'm sick of this!"

At this point, I become very much aware of myself. I think to myself: "I shouldn't be getting so angry." . . .

Once I'm outside, I break down crying, and I can't stop. I cry until I can't cry anymore—until I'm mentally and physically exhausted. Then I start to feel guilty about what I've just done . . . Then I think: "I'm a failure as a mother. I'm a lousy wife. My family would be better off without me."[29]

Alice, a 36-year-old data analyst, describes how her life would be different if she didn't have PMS:

I think that I would be a lot more successful. I'd be a better mother. I'd be a better wife. I'd be a better friend. I'd be better at my job. I'd be better all around. But what happens now is that I start getting these little bits and pieces together and then this stuff comes and scatters it all around. Then I've got to go and pick up all the pieces again. Sometimes I feel good, and then I think to myself, "OK, good, let's go! I'm ready to get organized and moving." Then a few days (sometimes even a few hours) later everything fizzles. All my energy is gone. I begin to feel like a lousy mother, wife, and friend.[30]

Teresa tells her story this way:

I really am a good mom. But during those days, I don't know how my kids can stand to be around me . . .

Sometimes, I can do it all. I make sure that all the things they need for school are ready on time. I also drive the carpool, and I'm a room mother at school. I make sure that they get to their lessons, and I pick them up from practice. I make sure that their diets are well balanced. I'm even a friend to their friends. You might say I'm everybody's favorite mother—during my good times.

But then I turn into an ogre, and it makes their heads spin . . . My husband can become alarmed at my behavior and step in. If I'm screaming, he tells me to calm down. If the kids need to be taken somewhere, he takes them. He takes the kids to the backyard or another room—anywhere else—to remove them. He's like a buffer zone. He says to the kids, "She'll be OK. She's just upset now. Let's go outside and play for a while." He creates diversions.

My reactions to my husband are mixed. In the past, I resented it if he stepped in . . . And then I would confront him with, "You're treating me like I'm an incompetent mother.". . . [Now] I feel like my husband has helped me identify a real problem.[31]

Maureen explains her relief at being diagnosed:

About 7 years ago, things started going wrong. I became extremely restless and unhappy with my life. I got divorced, quit one career, and started another. But it seemed that I was becoming less—not more—content. It took me quite a while to find out that my problem might be PMS. When I did find out, I jumped at the opportunity to learn as much as possible because I didn't like the person I was becoming. I was tremendously relieved to find out that I was not going through some incurable depression, but that I had something treatable.[32]

When I suggested to Bender that perhaps anger, depression, and exhaustion were actually reasonable responses to these women's circumstances, she was circumspect. "There's no question that women today are doing dual roles more than at any other time in history," she says. "But the fact is, she may feel very different as far as her energy level and capabilities [are concerned], depending on her cycle. At one point she may say, Of course, I'm doing too much. I got up, got the kids to day care, went to work, picked the kids up, made dinner, did the laundry, put the kids to bed, cleaned the house, and fell into bed. That is too much." But Bender says a non-PMS-ing woman can usually acknowledge that and then go on with her life, whereas the PMS sufferer "ends up in desperate despair." "The world doesn't change when we have PMS, our perspective does," she concludes.

And how is it that we, as a society, have come to privilege one "perspective" over another? As Sharon Golub, psychologist and past president of the Society for Menstrual Cycle Research, observes in her 1992 book *Periods*, any change in mood is now perceived as problematic. "Rather than accepting the cyclic changes as the norm," Golub explains, "some baseline from which we are not expected to deviate becomes the norm."[33] Golub, who has conducted many studies on the topic of menstruation and reviewed the findings of many more, takes a broad and judicious approach to the significance of PMS. Numerous studies have revealed that minor mood swings that women might ordinarily attribute to an event—"My boss was such an asshole today"—are instead attributed to hormones—"Work today was such a nightmare, I think I'm PMS."

"Women overstate the changes in their bodies that occur

during the course of the menstrual cycle," Golub explains. "And when they think that they are premenstrual, they report more problems than when they think they are mid-cycle." She speculates that menstruation reminds women of their bodies. "And most women are not particularly happy with their bodies."[34]

Which is not to say that women aren't genuinely feeling more stressed premenstrually. Many are. In several studies conducted between 1976 and 1989, researchers documented a loose connection between stress and PMS. In a 1979 study published in the *Journal of Human Stress*, 244 female college students filled out two separate questionnaires: one asked about changes in their lives over the past year and the other asked about menstrual symptoms. Those who reported more negative events in their life also reported more symptoms of PMS. The authors saw two ways of interpreting the data. Does stress make women more prone to menstrual pain (as it makes one more likely to succumb to illness)? Or does a stressed-out person have less tolerance for the same level of pain?[35]

While many reputable studies have shown a connection between a woman's moods—feeling more anxious or depressed premenstrually—and her cycles, Golub suggests we need to put this in perspective. As two of her 1976 studies—one published in the *Journal of Personality and Social Psychology* and the other in *Psychosomatic Medicine*—showed, the elevation in anxiety levels premenstrually was minor, less than that of college freshmen at orientation.[36] Similarly, research published in the journal *Social Science Research* in 1977 showed a greater fluctuation in mood over the course of a week than that reported over the menstrual cycle, with depression and anxiety peaking on Tuesdays and good cheer peaking, naturally, on Fridays. These mood cycles were observed in women *and* men.[37] And while weekly peaks and valleys were found to be greater than those reported over the menstrual cycle, very little time, energy, or money has been devoted to "cures" for these distressing mood swings. What this early research has showed us—and contemporary research has not disproved—is that the link between moods and menstrual cycles is subtle—not pathological—and that moods are more likely exaggerated by events than by a woman's menstrual cycle.

The fact is that, despite the rash of studies, we don't seem to know very much about PMS. For example, theories about the psychological origins of PMS are all over the map. In the 1930s, psychoanalyst Karen Horney said that women who suffered from cyclical mood swings were childless working women who were unconsciously denying their natural feminine desire for a child—and therefore suffered each month at the manifestation of failed pregnancy. By the 1970s, studies like psychologist Karen Paige's, published in *Psychology Today*, were suggesting the opposite: that the most conservative and religious women, who believed that a woman's place was in the home and who had no outside career ambitions, were the ones most likely to suffer from their periods.[38]

Clearly, there are various spins one can put on the statistics. For example, many women with PMS report food cravings. One 1969 study conducted on three hundred nurses discovered that those who had serious food cravings premenstrually also had more feelings of depression premenstrually.[39] Today, findings like these are used to suggest that a nutritional deficiency, say a lack of carbohydrates, is affecting mood, so that the women who have food cravings report more feelings of depression. But what if the reasons are sociological rather than physical? What if women who responded to food cravings felt depressed because after they ate, they felt fat? Who frames the research? Who owns the statistics? Who spins the stories?

THE PROZAC CURE

Consider 44-year-old Shelly Smith (not her real name). When I spoke with her, she described herself as an at-home mother of three school-age children, a doctor's wife, and a volunteer at a hospice for the dying. She also identified herself as a PMS sufferer. In August of 1995, fearing that her marriage was on the rocks and finding her PMS-related depression nearly insurmountable, she began taking Prozac every month during the week before her period started. The drug changed her life. "It worked so immediately and so well," she tells me, flipping through a journal to reference the exact dates she began on what is formally known as a selective serotonin reuptake inhibitor (SSRI). "Here," she says, reading aloud the shorthand entries that tracked her mood:

August 24, Thursday: Feeling very low and unappreciated at home. Victimized. Hold together for hospice visit. Things fall apart at home. Tears and arguments. Want to escape kids.

August 25, Friday: Start Prozac in a.m. Feel a bit fuzzy mid-afternoon but normal by evening. No tears or quick anger. Met with Linda. [Aside: "That's our therapist. We were in couples counseling."]

August 26, Saturday: Period began. No quick anger or frustration. Dinner out with friends.

In September, the cycle repeated itself:

September 12, Tuesday: Couldn't get dinner together. Picked up Taco Bell and TV dinners. Stayed in my room. Wanted to avoid life. But not too depressed yet. Heading downhill, though. Want a sick day. Just want everybody to leave me alone and have a sick day.

September 13, Wednesday: Don't want to participate in life. Still agonizing over work decisions. [Aside: "I was thinking about getting a part-time job."] Day 18 of my cycle. I decided that today was the appropriate day to start [Prozac].

September 14, Thursday: I did volunteer work all day. Felt good. Positive. No stress, anxiety or feeling like a failure.

Smith concludes the month's journal entries by observing that her feelings, on Prozac, were now "normal and appropriate." Visits to the couples counselor ceased, and life was once again manageable.

Prozac was clearly superior to the cures she had tried in the past. Over the years, Smith had tried everything from low-dose birth control pills to vitamin supplements to vitamin B_6 to eliminating salt and sugar from her diet. None of these things worked. Instead, things got worse. Initially, PMS had made her "edgy," "sad," "angry," and "out of control" for just a few days right before her period; eventually she was feeling this way more than half the month. Like most women who report suffering from PMS, that feeling of being "out of control" was the most frightening aspect of the illness.

And this had been going on for nearly ten years, explains Smith. Like many women with PMS, Smith began to get PMS symptoms "somewhere in the middle of having children." That's when she suddenly found herself losing patience, yelling at her kids, yelling at her husband. "Eventually I felt like I was premenstrual more than I was not," she says. "And it was getting pretty destructive to my relationship with my husband. I was PMS so much of the time that there was not enough time to heal and get back on track before it was back."

Smith pauses, carefully searching for the sequence of events. "Things [had been] deteriorating between us for about a year when my husband, who is a physician, mentioned to me one day that they're using Prozac for PMS and maybe I should try it." Smith hastens to add that she found the suggestion reprehensible at first. "My reaction was 'I'm not going to be your Stepford Wife.' I just didn't feel like he should be the one controlling me and my emotions." Smith eventually opted to consult a marriage counselor as a way of addressing some of the problems in her relationship with her husband. But the PMS mood swings persisted. Finally, when another friend mentioned reading about Prozac as a treatment for PMS, Smith relented and asked her husband to write her out a prescription for the drug.

"It worked so immediately and so well," Smith recalls. "It wasn't like a happy pill. Just a sense of being in control and not going to the extremes of emotion. I didn't feel dulled. I just didn't feel so edgy and I was not overreacting to things."

Her life began to turn around. "My husband was thrilled," she says. Even her kids were relieved. "I'd say, 'Have you noticed I don't seem so hysterical?' and they're appreciative."

For Smith, recalling those dark days now takes some effort. Trying to convey, for the uninitiated, just what makes PMS so frightening, she says: "I was flying off the handle, overreacting. It doesn't seem like you're overreacting, of course." She pauses, thinking. "It seems like the rest of the world is wrong, and if they'd only listen to you they'd realize." She gives a quiet, self-deprecating laugh.

As readers are probably well aware, Prozac took the country by storm in 1988. So much so that by the time a picture of the drug ran on the cover of Newsweek in March 1990, more than 650,000 prescriptions were being filled a month. It was the fastest-growing psychotherapeutic medicine ever. Later, the Detroit News described SSRIs such as Prozac and Zoloft as the 1990s version of "Mother's Little Helper" and reported that 38.6 million prescriptions were being written annually for SSRIs in this country, "a 100 percent increase from 1994, six years after Prozac first came on the market in the United States." By 1997, the global market for antidepressants was creeping toward $6 billion, with sales for Prozac alone topping $2 billion.

But even with millions of Americans already on board, pharmaceutical giants like Eli Lilly and Pfizer, makers of Prozac and Zoloft, were still hustling for new clients. And often that meant going straight to the patients via text-heavy ads that ran in popular magazines from *Glamour* to *Parenting*. After listing the symptoms of depression—trouble sleeping, difficulty concentrating, loss of appetite, lack of energy—Lilly's 1998 "Prozac Can Help" ad campaign reminds women that "Prozac has been prescribed for more than 17 million Americans. Chances are someone you know is blossoming again because of it." (According to the National Institute of Mental Health, women are twice as likely as men to have depression—or at least to seek help and be treated for it; women also take two-thirds of all antidepressants prescribed today.) Part of Lilly's "altruistic" motive, of course, is to help identify those suffering from depression who haven't yet realized they *ought* to be patients.

If there weren't enough depressed Americans out there, well then, they'd recruit some. In an effort to help the reticent realize that they (or a loved one) might be in trouble, pharmaceutical companies organize mental health days. In a trenchant June 1996 *Harper's* cover story on the "new age of pharmo-capitalism," Greg Critser reported on one such mental health day. "Under the auspices of the American Psychiatric Association and funded by Lilly, 56,000 attendees in all fifty states were 'screened' for depression. Organizers bragged that 'more than 50 percent of attendees scored positive for depression and were referred.'"

The drug companies also targeted health-management groups and HMOs, peddling SSRIs as a panacea that would keep per-patient costs down. "Almost immediately, the average number of insurer-paid visits to talk therapists fell dramatically while drug-therapy numbers soared," Critser reported. "By the late eighties, of nearly 16 million patients who visited doctors for depression, 70 percent ended up in drug therapy."

Clearly SSRIs have proved a boon to insurers as well as to the pharmaceutical companies that manufacture them. Today they are being prescribed for everything from calming hyperactive children to enhancing public-speaking skills in adults. Is it any wonder that the manufacturers are anxious to test the efficacy of these drugs on additional disorders?

In June 1995, Dr. Meir Steiner did just that. He conducted a study and then published an article in the *New England Journal of Medicine* announcing that he'd found an effective cure for PMS: Prozac. Conducting a test on several hundred women at seven Canadian clinics, he discovered a 50-to-75-percent improvement in the symptoms of women who took a daily dose of Prozac.[40]

Prozac and its sister drugs, such as Zoloft, work by keeping the brain from suctioning up too much serotonin. Serotonin is the medium through which messages travel between neural transmitters and receivers, and a lack of serotonin is believed to negatively affect mood. Though no one seems quite sure what serotonin has to do with fluctuating hormones or a woman's menstrual cycle, SSRIs seem to benefit PMS sufferers.

In effect, Steiner provided a rationale for the drugs that general practitioners and gynecologists had already been prescribing for nearly a decade. They now had *proof* that PMS sufferers improved with Prozac. While FDA approval could still take years, it's of little consequence. Physicians will simply continue to prescribe the drug for this "off-label" use — as they've been doing all along. And since research into the effects of SSRIs on PMS is limited, doctors use their own judgment about prescribing it: some have patients take it all through the month; others tell women to take it when they feel a PMS flare-up coming on.

And why not? The solution makes everybody happy. Doctors get patients in and out of the office faster; insurance companies prefer it as a simpler—certainly cheaper—substitution for endless talk therapy; and drug companies get a whole new "client caste" (to crib a term from Ehrenreich and English).

While 42 percent of the patients who entered Steiner's study did not complete it—many assigned to take the placebo complained of its lack of efficacy, and many taking the Prozac complained of its side effects—the doctor preferred to focus on the positive. He told the *Calgary Herald* that when the study was finished, a number of women begged him to keep giving them the drug because their lives had returned to normal for the first time in many years. "They were pleading; their husbands were pleading and saying, 'Whatever you gave her, keep her on it.'"

Prozac defenders quickly dismiss any suggestions that the drug is "Mother's Little Helper." Jean Endicott, the director of the Premenstrual Evaluation Unit at Columbia-Presbyterian Hospital and a professor of clinical psychology at Columbia-Presbyterian's College of Physicians and Surgeons, echoes Dalton's proof-of-the-pudding's-in-the-progesterone argument exactly, except that her proof's in the Prozac: "I don't think it's very helpful to say you're just drugging the women," Endicott says. "I mean, the women will vote with their feet. If they think it's helpful, it's their decision to make." Going beyond Endicott's argument, Meir Steiner, author of the Canadian study proving Prozac cured PMS, plays up his impressive statistics. He plays down the source of funding for his research on the topic: Eli Lilly & Company, makers of Prozac.

Was PMS simply another example of drug companies exaggerating a problem so that they could then offer a highly lucrative solution? Perhaps. But the groundwork for treating PMS as a disease was laid in July of 1993 when the American Psychiatric Association, after prolonged debate, formally included it in the fourth edition of its *Diagnostic and Statistical Manual*. Naming the disease Premenstrual Dysphoric Disorder, the APA's decision to include it—albeit in an appendix rather than in the body of the book—marked an important turning point in the way the medical establishment viewed PMS. Because the *Diagnostic and Statistical Manual* functions as the psychiatric profession's dictionary of disorders and symptoms, the APA clearly sets an agenda, helping to define which illnesses insurance companies will cover and what government agencies and private foundations will spend research dollars on.

The debate surrounding PMS's inclusion in the *Manual* was a heated one. "There was concern on both sides," says Dr. Nada Stotland, who chaired the Association's Committee on Women and served on the working committee charged with recommending whether or not to include PMDD in the manual. "There's a cadre of clinicians and researchers but also lay women who say, 'I suffer from these terrible symptoms—why doesn't the medical community pay any attention?' Then there's a cadre of women that say, 'If you label women by their hormones, you tar everyone with the same brush and make us susceptible to discrimination in jobs and the culture at large.'"

One of the inherent problems of such working committees is that they are appropriately staffed with "experts"—and those "experts" tend to be people who have researched and been published on the disease, i.e., those with a vested interest in its existence. (Recall also that much of these medical experts' research is funded by pharmaceutical companies, which are looking for "cures" they can manufacture and sell; questioning the very existence of the disease would hardly be profitable for a researcher.) Such experts dominated the PMDD committee, though some token skeptics like Nada Stotland were also included.

"There is data to show that most women and men in this society believe that women have adverse behavioral and emotional effects from the menstrual cycle, especially premenstrually," Stotland says. Indeed, one of the classic studies of this phenomenon was conducted on forty-four female Princeton undergraduates who were told that a new technique—analyzing their brain waves—could determine exactly when their periods would start. They were then given an arbitrary day. Those who thought their periods were imminent reported more pain, water retention, and eating-habit changes than those who were told their periods were weeks away.[41] Another study, conducted by the World Health Organization in 1981 and described in *The Economist,* some years later, showed radical differences in the ways different cultures experienced PMS. In Indonesia, only 23 percent of women described themselves as having premenstrual mood changes like irritability, lethargy, and depression. In the former Yugoslavia, 73 percent of women said they had these symptoms premenstrually. The study concluded that "socially mediated expectations and beliefs determine the incidence of premenstrual symptoms."[42]

"Science and data, especially about symptoms and behaviors, are very dependent on social context," Stotland says. "And that makes it far more difficult to define what is a disease and what isn't a disease." PMS is "unique in so far as it's a syndrome that the whole society thinks exists and that the whole society thinks afflicts most women," she explains. "Girls don't grow up thinking, If I'm female I will grow up and have schizophrenia. But they do think, If I'm female I will grow up and have PMS. Unlike any other disorder in the manual, more people will insist they have it than will turn out to have it. It's a disorder that people are eager to claim they have." That makes for substantial methodological difficulties. "When the whole society is eager to ascribe anything problematic in a woman's feelings or behavior to the menstrual cycle, you've got to be extremely careful."

Stotland suggested to her fellow committee members that they look very closely at gender roles. Referring to some of the scariest symptoms PMS sufferers report—"anger," "aggression," "feeling out of control"—she suggests that it may be premature to classify them as a disease. "With men, our society sanctions having tantrums, expressing rage, being aggressive, and that's considered to be a normal concomitant of all the responsibility and leadership they have," she says. "And yet women are expected to absorb all that. And if on several days of the month she should have difficulty doing that, she might say she's 'out of control.' She may say she is PMS." According to Stotland, the woman may want that diagnosis and treatment.

Because she may not like being that way and she gets in trouble for being that way.

But another committee member, Jean Endicott, says that this doesn't make sense, "because not every woman who has a stressful life develops PMDD." Dr. Leah Dickstein, the director of the Division of Attitudinal and Behavioral Medicine at the University of Louisville's Department of Psychiatry and a clinician who treats women with PMDD, goes even further in her endorsement of the idea of PMDD, insisting that *not* including PMDD in the manual would stigmatize women. "After all, it's important for women to know that they have real symptoms that are diagnosable," she says. "And those women need recognition, so they can get treatment. There has to be a category so they can get reimbursed, and so that it's clear it's not a figment of one woman's imagination."

One of the compromises the committee floated was to include qualifiers that could be applied to any diagnosis in the manual—for example, "worse premenstrually" or "worse in adolescent boys"—rather than treating PMDD as a freestanding illness, which would make it seem as if a woman's hormones are a disease and a man's hormones aren't. Currently, the *DSM* does this with postpartum depression. Instead of having a whole separate category, they have a qualifier: a woman has depression "with post-partum onset." Although there is an ongoing dispute about this "disease" as well.

The committee went back and forth. Members talked to experts, debated each other, and examined roughly four hundred studies and research papers, mostly on PMS. And they worried. Some committee members were concerned that labeling PMDD a disorder (which is what the *DSM* had labeled homosexuality until 1973) would stigmatize all women. Although the *DSM* differentiates between PMS—the mild bloating, breast tenderness, fatigue, anger, etc., that many women experience—and PMDD, which it defines as a far more debilitating depression, some committee psychiatrists worried that the public would collapse these distinctions. Others insisted that this was exactly why the committee was obligated to include a careful definition of PMDD and its symptoms.

Finally, there were those who weren't convinced that a persuasive case had been made to declare either PMS or PMDD a disorder. "Women are often paid less, put in subordinate positions, occasionally beaten up at home, and nowadays have to earn a significant portion of the family income and be responsible for the home, where they do the lion's share of the work—and still they are asked not to be angry and always be in control," says Stotland. "So all of those things don't mean there's no such thing as PMDD, but that it's very hard to establish hormones as the cause of these feelings."

In fact, a recent study, presented at the Society for Menstrual Cycle Research's 1995 conference in Montreal, tested the implications of "naming" the disease. Concerned that much of the PMS research out there was methodologically flawed—subjects were almost always aware that menstruation was the topic of the study and women were asked to retrospectively map out their emotions over the course of the month—Heather Nash and Joan Chrisler devised a different test. They told 134 introductory psychology students, men and women, that they were conducting a study on "psychology and personal insight." First they gave them a questionnaire listing more than fifty typical PMS symptoms, such as impaired concentration, change in appetite, feelings of being overwhelmed, and lethargy. The students did not know they were responding to the standard "menstrual distress questionnaire" that psychologists and doctors use to determine the presence of PMS. Two weeks later, the students were given part II of the test, which included a segment quoting the *DSM* definition of PMS and its symptoms. Half the students got the real definition; half the students got the real definition with "Episodic Dysphoric Disorder" substituted as the name of the illness. They were asked if anyone they knew suffered from these symptoms, or if they did. Not surprisingly, plenty of students identified males who suffered from this "disorder" when it was defined as "Episodic Dysphoric Disorder." (Several female students even identified their boyfriends as suffering from it.) And male participants were more likely to say that they suffered from it when it was described that way. When the exact same symptoms were labeled as PMS, the women were more likely to indicate they suffered from it; men, of course, were quite certain they did not. Nash and Chrisler say their research shows that "gender-neutral emotions like tension, anxiety, irritability, and anger become woman-only symptoms as soon as they fall under the title of a menstrual cycle disorder." Though proponents of including PMS in the *DSM* say there is no reason to think a disease that affects only women will be generalized into a disease affecting all women, Nash and Chrisler say their research indicates otherwise. "The results demonstrate that knowledge of the diagnosis not only affects the way women view their own premenstrual experiences, but influences the attributions that men and women make in explaining both the experience of certain changes in mood and physiology and the behavior of women in general." They insist that "what many of the proponents of the diagnosis are failing to address is the social context in which this diagnosis is being applied."[43]

But ultimately these reservations were dismissed. In the end, the APA—with a panel of 17 men and 4 women—voted to formally include the disease in the appendix, under the heading "Mood Disorders Not Otherwise Specified." In a July 8, 1993, *Washington Post* article, University of Toronto psychology professor Paula Caplan describes this as a bribe: "The APA says, 'We'll believe what you women tell us about how you're feeling—but you've got to let us call you mentally ill.'"

PMS and the Remaking of the Self

In some ways, tossing Prozac into the PMDD debate only shores up the arguments for the existence of the disease. For most doctors, researchers, and psychiatrists, the pairing of PMS and Prozac is a win-win situation. The reasoning goes thus: If a woman complains of having PMS and gets better by taking Prozac, then PMS must be biologically based because it responds to drugs like Prozac. This is something Peter D. Kramer talks about in his 1993 best-seller *Listening to Prozac*. Noting that a tremendous number of people who would not previously have been classified as clinically depressed or as obsessive-compulsive or as suffering from an anxiety disorder get better on Prozac, he says we are changing our definition of disease. "We as a society will have to decide how comfortable we are with using chemicals to modify personality in useful, attractive ways," he writes. "We may mask the issue by defining less and less severe mood states as pathology, in effect saying, 'If it responds to an antidepressant, it's depression.' Already, it seems to me, psychiatric diagnosis had been subject to a sort of 'diagnostic bracket creep'—the expansion of categories to match the scope of relevant medications."[44]

Though Kramer mentions PMS only in passing—as one of the many mood disorders treated with Prozac—his musings on the topic sound much like the Psychiatric Association's PMDD discussion. Kramer, of course, comes down firmly in defense of Prozac. But along the way he pauses to worry about patients to whom one wouldn't ordinarily prescribe drugs. Kramer heard his patients on Prozac describe themselves as "better than well." If they had been only moderately unhappy before, was this drug necessary? That is, was Prozac acting as a cure or as an enhancer? Calling this "cosmetic psychopharmacology," he detailed the lives of some of his patients—mostly women, it seems—who had problems that miraculously disappeared once they began taking Prozac.

One of his patients, Julia, approached him after reading a magazine article he'd written about Prozac. At first, he reports, "I was less impressed with any sign of mood disorder than with her frustration at work and home." He describes Julia as a mother of several children who worked a part-time job at a nursing home and "demanded extraordinary control at home," insisting that the beds be made perfectly, the children be tidy, etc. "Julia's husband was uncomfortable with her inflexibility, and she found herself raising her voice to him and the children more than was right," Kramer explains. "Also, the nursing-home job was beneath the level of her abilities." She wanted more challenge but felt trapped. "How could she manage her tasks in the house and at the same time tackle a more demanding job?"[45]

Julia's gynecologist diagnosed Julia's depression as PMS. Kramer saw Julia's problem as perfectionism. "Perhaps Julia almost met the criteria [for Obsessive-Compulsive Disorder]: there were weeks when she did two loads of laundry every day; if the floors were dirty, she might stay up late to wash them," Kramer writes, putting forward a description that's dangerously close to pegging every housewife with young kids as suffering from OCD.

A social worker whom Julia was seeing described the case differently, calling it "gender-role conflict." The social worker speculated that, "identifying with her father, Julia secretly, or even unconsciously, felt herself to be more competent than her spouse—at the same time, not least for her own sense of security, she wanted to maintain the illusion that her husband was like her father, strong and decisive." She insisted that Julia's paralyzing unhappiness was "an expression of inner conflict over control in the family."[46]

Ultimately Kramer gave Julia the drug she had come to him requesting: Prozac. She reported that she was "transformed"; her husband "had nothing but good things to say about the effect of the drug . . . so unused had he been over the years to having a wife who could sit with him of an evening without being jumpy and critical."[47]

In the end, the same problem was diagnosed differently by each of the three "experts" in Julia's life—her social worker, her psychiatrist, and her gynecologist. Her social worker saw genuine conflict and problems in Julia's life. Her therapist, Kramer, thought her expectations for control were too high to be "normal." Her gynecologist saw the problems as insignificant and her extreme responses as hormonally based; he diagnosed her disease as PMS.

In the provocative concluding chapter to his book, titled "The Message in the Capsule," Kramer quotes a colleague, Richard Schwartz, who worries about Prozac's use—and overuse—as a mood brightener. Schwartz contrasts the attitude of American psychiatrists who will prescribe antidepressants for "prolonged bereavement," which they define as lasting more than one year, with the custom in Greece, where loss of a spouse, parent, or child typically entails a formal grieving period of five years. "When doctors pharmacologically mitigate the pain of bereavement after one year, they may be using medication to reinforce cultural norms and encourage conformity," Kramer speculates. "The medication seems to justify the standard that is in place by labeling those who deviate from a cultural norm as ill and then 'curing' them." In the end, of course, Kramer comes down in defense of Prozac, but he tempers his endorsement with some disturbing questions, questions that have an eerie resonance when applied to treatment for PMS. "How large a sphere of human problems we choose to define as medical is an important social decision," he writes. "But words like 'choose' and 'decision' perhaps misstate the process. It is easy to imagine that our role will be passive, that as a society we will in effect permit the material technology, medications, to define what is health and what is illness."[48]

Hormones or Circumstance?
Medical Solutions for Social Problems

"PMS is physiological; that's the point," says Dr. Leah Dickstein. After studying and treating women with PMS for years, she is quite certain. "These women's symptoms are real and repetitive and treatable. Exercise helps some people, watching diet helps some people, but some need medication." There's no doubt in Dickstein's mind that Prozac is curing a definite illness. "It's like a miracle drug," she says.

Like each of the psychiatrists and doctors I talk to who prescribe SSRIs, Dickstein is thrilled with the results and mentions that the side effects are negligible. (Even those like Nada Stotland, who question the very existence of PMDD, aren't alarmed at the use of Prozac, since, Dr. Stotland says, it's harmless enough and is probably helping women who are genuinely depressed, though they may have been misdiagnosed as having PMDD.) As to whether Prozac is simply the 1990s version of "Mother's Little Helper," Dickstein says that's absurd. "That's derogatory toward women," she insists. "It doesn't make sense. If you didn't need it, you wouldn't use it. And hopefully physicians and psychiatrists are ethical enough not to prescribe what's not needed."

Yet most people who are diagnosed as suffering from depression still do some cursory introspection, making a trip or two to the therapist to ask, "Why do I feel this way?" A woman whose gynecologist or family doctor prescribes Prozac for PMS may not even get *that* far. (And 80 percent of the new Prozac prescriptions written for women were written by doctors other than psychiatrists.) The problem is physical. End of subject.

The beauty of a "syndrome" is its sweeping nature. It's a collection of problems that experts have coalesced into a group. And given a name. For easier classification. And because a syndrome is a collection of symptoms, its existence is open to interpretation, which is why anecdotes are used to substantiate the existence of PMS as a disorder. Yet as *proof* of PMS, these anecdotes seem no more persuasive than the pathology of the uterus that doctors once used to explain away a similar host of problems. Even the snippets of the lives offered up as proof in Kramer's book, in Dalton's book, in Bender and Kelleher's book, couched in arguments to persuade me otherwise, make me skeptical. I see a host of reasons—quite legitimate ones—for PMS sufferers to be responding angrily and aggressively; responses that may indeed be "normal and appropriate" rather than "overreacting." With deft sleight of hand, it is as easy to pin these women's anger on circumstance as on hormones. Which is what makes syndromes and the anecdotes that substantiate them such useful tools. They're so malleable in the right hands.

To that end, let me throw an anecdote of mine into the mix. It is so easy with things as impalpable—and open to interpretation—as hormones and moods to spin events.

In the early morning hours of November 14, 1996, I wandered the maternity ward of New York's Beth Israel Hospital, sobbing. About twenty-four hours earlier, I had given birth to a baby boy. Now a nurse comforted me, telling me to calm down, to relax, that my hormones were going crazy, that this was "postpartum." I let her lead me back to my bed and dutifully climbed in. I tried to stop crying, but as I went over events in my head, I just got madder—and cried more.

The delivery, by a kind and competent doctor, had been a normal vaginal delivery. That is to say, it was still long, grueling, and painful. By the time my episiotomy was stitched up and I was moved from the labor-and-delivery floor to the maternity ward, it was approximately 5 a.m. I had not slept in over 48 hours.

For the next two days, my recovery would be hindered, not helped, by my hospital sojourn. I began to feel doomed to my own little circle of sleepless hell. For many reasons: (1) An intercom above my head would crackle with announcements at irregular intervals—day and night—usually in an effort to locate one of the nurses on this severely understaffed ward. (2) After three days of exhausting labor, when I could have most used the support of my partner, he was banned from spending the night in my room. That meant (3) I was left alone with a newborn who wanted to nurse constantly, probably because he was not nursing properly. (4) Calls for assistance went unanswered. (5) An understaffed hospital cut corners by having lots of aides and few trained nurses. Though I am supposed to wait for an aide to help me get to the bathroom—I'm still attached to an IV pole and they like to make sure your epidural has completely worn off and you can walk properly—no one came when I rang once . . . twice . . . three times. After an hour, I struggled to the bathroom on my own. (6) At 3 a.m., a squalling baby became the battleground between a nursery staff that wanted to suggest a bottle and official hospital policy, which pushed breast-feeding. (7) The maternity ward had no hot water. Aside from having to douche my episiotomy stitches with freezing-cold water (the doctor recommends this water rinse over scraping toilet paper over the raw flesh), I was desperate

for a hot shower to rinse off blood, sweat, and . . . whatever. I had
not bathed since giving birth more than twenty-four hours earlier,
and there was nothing I wanted more right then. As I wandered
the halls at 7 a.m., warm water struck me as an eminently reasonable request. But there was no hot water to be had.

What do I do? I start crying. *Why* do I start crying?

To my mind I am crying because I am pissed. I am wander-
ing the halls of a maternity ward I have paid handsomely for
the privilege of visiting, checking the water temperature in
each of the available showers, finding them dirty and cold,
hoping no one's noticing the blood leaking down my leg, and
weeping in frustration. A nurse finds me. She tells me the hot
water in this wing doesn't work but she'll take me to another
wing of the hospital. We check another wing. We cannot find a
working shower. That's when the nurse tells me my hormones
are going crazy—that old postpartum thing—not to worry.

I find that comforting. For a moment. But I don't really feel
"sad." I am mad. I'm angry to be stuck in a shitty hospital. I am
trapped, dependent on the kindness of strangers (which is not
forthcoming) and indignant that in 1997, in one of the richest
countries in the world, with one of the costliest health-care systems, I am stuck in an unsanitary, understaffed, dilapidated,
disorganized, and dysfunctional maternity ward. I am angry
because it doesn't have to be that way.

But I give up and take a cold shower. After lunch a nurse–
social worker visits me. (I am convinced the nurse who comforted me in the morning told her to check up on me: "You've
got a live one in bed B," or whatever.) She kindly helps me
with the breast-feeding and, when I tell her my complaints
about the hospital, I grow weepy again. She, like a succession

of supervisors who will visit me in the aftermath, behaves as though she's never heard these complaints before. Surely I'm not the first woman to discover there is no hot water here? (Four months later, I will run into a woman with a newborn at my pediatrician's office. We get to chatting about labor and delivery, and she complains that the hospital she was in last week—Beth Israel—had no hot water on the maternity ward.) But the nurse soothes me. She too tells me about my hormones going haywire. She also tells me that this can be a very stressful time.

Both are probably true. The real question is, how will we, as a society, weigh this kind of experience? We could explain my behavior away by saying my postpartum hormones were wreaking havoc—which probably has *some* truth to it—or we could decide that the reasons that pushed me over the edge were in fact legitimate reasons for a person to feel angry or out of control and reflected some systemic problems in the way the hospital handled birth and delivery. PMS, like postpartum depression, can be played either way. In America today, we've chosen to diagnose the problem as hormones. We've decided to tip the balance toward the physiological because potions and cures are easier to come by than social transformation.

Which is not to suggest that the women whose anecdotes I've detailed here aren't suffering. Clearly they are. But if a confluence of factors—biological, environmental, and cultural—is contributing to their symptoms, then perhaps the importance we've attached to each is askew.

Certainly the solutions such problems engender are troubling: (1) Read a self-help book, which implies that the problem is with *you*, not with a sexist culture that hands you multiple frustrations at work and then a second shift at home. The advice pushes self-control — eat different foods, exercise more, etc. — and implies that you must change your behavior, not your situation. (2) Take a drug (progesterone) to get yourself under control. Or (3) take another drug (Prozac) to modify your perspective.

The American Psychiatric Association's decision to consider PMDD a disorder is a particularly telling example of what's at stake. By making cycles of anger and sadness a "disease," they're defining the norm — an even-keeled, no-peaks-no-valleys existence — for us. The refrain that sticks with me, encountered over and over again in all the PMS literature, is women's desperate fear of "being out of control." In our rush to categorize, is it possible we've misidentified the problem? Or identified an aspect of it but missed its essential qualities? PMS sufferers describe being unable to control their anger, and therefore their daily lives and interactions. Aside from the fact that anger is a decidedly unfeminine trait, and therefore frightening, it could be that their anger has a legitimate source. But it's also true that the solutions are "out of their control." If the stresses that push them over the edge have to do with obediently playing the cards a sexist culture has dealt them, facing power imbalances on the job and in the home, and continuing an exhausting effort to juggle both with grace and humor — and minimal support from the government and the larger culture — then it is no wonder that so many women get "moody." Perhaps feeling "out of control" is a reasonable response to their circumstances: they *are* out of control because the solutions to their problems need to be social. The private solutions they can see are indeed nonsolutions. And the hope that a social movement would provide is as absent as the movement itself. (Hope arrives instead in the form of carbohydrate beverages, oil of evening primrose, progesterone, and Prozac.)

In some ways, it seems that women, after a brief personal-is-political interlude in the 1960s, are being encouraged to see the problems and stresses in their lives as isolated. They can come together as a community only in confessional PMS support groups, which rely on a medical model and a self-help formula that puts the fault squarely on their female selves, saying that if they only exercised a little self-control—and changed their diet, and organized their lives, and exerted more willpower, and triumphed over food cravings, and exercised every day—they could "manage" this chronic illness. And if they just can't, then they should take this pill.

Of course, I am returning to an old, though currently unfashionable, idea: blaming women's anger on PMS lets society off the hook.

PART FOUR

Unlikely Prophets:

The Menstrual Counterculture

Your body understood it on the day you were born. There is a bigger plan in life. And every month you are reminded that you play a part. It is nothing more than a period. And nothing less than a force of nature.

The inSync miniform works the way your body does—simply and naturally. It's held in place comfortably and securely by the gentle pressure of your body. Unlike pads, there are no adhesives. And unlike tampons, no insertion is necessary. It's small enough to fit in the palm of your hand, and provides all the absorption you may need for light flow. For a free trial offer, call toll free 1-888-8-inSync.

Actual size.

THE NEW CHOICE IN LIGHT FLOW PROTECTION

INSYNC
MINIFORMS

24 UNSCENTED MINIFORMS

While PMS is the most public of phenomena, normal, nonpathological periods remain a taboo topic. Still, there is some movement afoot to challenge the culture of concealment surrounding menstruation. A few women—and men—are troubled by the way we talk about periods and advocate a new menstrual health. Scattered signs of resistance surface on grrrl-power sites on the Web. And a few enlightened health educators and activists have written straightforward, nonclinical texts telling girls what they can expect when they bleed.

When it comes to adults, the harbingers of change are more elusive. I discovered only three: the Museum of Menstruation, a new menstrual products company, and a collection of goddess-feminists determined to celebrate their cycles. With the exception of the savvy cyber-grrrls, it was not a promising collection.

THE RESISTANCE: GRRRLS SPEAK OUT

On the Web, a thriving girl-power movement fluctuates between moments of unfocused rage—"Boys bite!"—and an often-sophisticated awareness of the package of products and lies that girls are being urged to buy. Signs that the "hygienic crisis" can be surmounted, that girls are not merely passive consumers of mainstream culture, crop up in 'zines, chat rooms, and personal Web sites, offering scattered glimpses of hope for the future. (One young woman urges girls to adopt an in-your-face attitude about bleeding and declares Ani DiFranco's "Blood in the Boardroom" the menstrual national anthem: "sitting in the boardroom/the i'm-so-bored room/listening to the suits talk about their world/i didn't really have much to say the whole time i was there/so i just left a big, brown bloodstain on their white chair.") A particularly revealing encounter between grrrls and the sanitary protection industry took place in 1996.

On the Web, gURL mag/zine (magzine.gurl.com), a funky on-line site created by three students in New York University's telecommunications program, operates in the finest grrrl-power tradition. Its articles run the gamut, and, with a light touch, assuage the fears of girls who worry that their bodies fall short of perfect. For example, one series, called "The Boob Files," features hilarious articles, my favorite being one titled "Every BOob-bearing Individual Knows That No Two BOobs Are Alike." ("Sometimes I wonder how it is that two bOobs could be so different, how could one be so distinguished and the other, so mediocre?" the author muses.) The magazine has a regular "You Do the Review" feature where girls are invited to visit a specific Web site, then to respond to it under a thumbs-up or thumbs-down graphic.

In August 1996, gURL directed its young readers' attention to troom (troom.com), the Tambrands Web site for teens. While the thumbs-up votes won (259 to 168), in the thumbs-down column there is a lively critique of Tambrands, the menstrual attitudes it peddles, and the facile methods it employs to sell products—and stereotypes.

What's got all these girls fuming that "the site BLOWS" and is "way cheesy besides"?

Created in February 1996 and maintained at a cost of

$300,000 a year, troom presents "Tina's room." Teenage Tina's bedroom is a jumble of objects visitors can click on. For example, girls put the cursor—a tampon-applicator icon—on Tina's diary in order to peruse her musings on adolescent life. A click on an interactive calendar lets girls keep track of their monthly cycles—so they're not taken by surprise! A mirror transports visitors to "Reflections," a list of questions and answers. ("Do you like a guy, and are not sure he's good for you?" the mirror reflects. Then, slipping into omniscient-expert mode, it answers its own question: "If your scope/boyfriend starts pressuring you to be something you're not, or to go faster in the relationship than you're ready for . . . HE'S NOT FOR YOU!!! . . . And if he really wants you to sleep with him and you're nowhere near ready, show him the door.") If girls click on the menstrual products casually displayed in Tina's top drawer, they can learn about the latest new Tambrands products, via perky little first-person notes ("Hi. I'm a 100% cotton tampon without an applicator that you insert easily with your finger," etc.). The girls get to order free samples. And Procter & Gamble has the opportunity to store and process their addresses, to use that information to contact the girls with future ads, and to sell its list to third parties. P&G also plants a "cookie" in the girls' hard drives, a file that monitors and records all the Web sites a girl visits so the company can get a handle on her interests and how to better plug its products to her. Tambrands brags that it had 100,000 free-sample requests in troom's first year.

With traffic to the site growing by 30 percent per month, Tambrands recently announced that it intended to begin selling *ad space* on troom.com. While this sounds incredible—how can one big walking advertisement sell ads?—the truth is that many of the naive young visitors to troom.com don't realize this is "sponsored content," as corporations like to call it. "It's a neat page and she's brave to share her personal stuff," one girl commented after visiting Tina's room. Another found it "pretty cool" but wondered, "Is it supposed to be about your period so much?" A third fan said she really liked troom.com but offered this criticism: "I think they have a bit of an obsession over tampons, though."

More astute critics responded: "People who think it talks about tampons too much: um, Hello, it's Tampax's website." The girls complain about Tina's frilly, fluffy girlishness ("so damn BARBIE"), about the condescending, didactic tone ("so mom-ish"), and about the assumption that girls are only into makeup and boys ("This girl is as shallow as a kiddie pool"). Insisting that the site makes them "wanna barf" and speculating that it was created by some fifty-year-old ad exec who "wears his wife's Wonder Bra while she's in the shower," the girls trash Tina's room.

They pick up on denigrating subtexts, like troom's "Supermodel of the Month" feature:

> It was feeding into that whole makeup industry crap. Like supermodel of the month?? PUHLEAZE. Who gives a damn? What have supermodels ever done to improve our planet, besides tell the rest of us our bodies are inadequate?

They dis the advice they're offered:

> Check this one out. It's so bad. "Boys don't like aggressive girls, so you shouldn't be one!" and so on. Blecch!

And, perhaps most encouraging, the girls were commenting on—and rejecting—the conventional pabulum about dating and sex:

> I can't really believe the advice given in the reflections section. It is pretty bad. I just read 3 reasons why you shouldn't make the first move. It made me cringe . . .

Finally, some girls found everything about Tina, this tired, trumped-up vision of femininity they were being fed, infuriating.

> I wish someone knew how to make a bomb disguised as a tampon so I could sneak into this girl's bathroom, switch her tampons with the bombs, and then watch from the outside as she explodes, sending her "pre-teen reproductive system" all over the fucking place.

Disgusted by the rampant commercialism and transparent agenda, an encouraging collection of girls emphatically declared troom "a waste of cyberspace."

But when they look for confirmation—"Are we all alone out here in thinking this is a load of crap?"—it's slim pickings. There are books out there trying to promote a new menstrual health among girls, but girls would have to be very lucky, or very determined, to discover them. (As I noted earlier, most puberty books tend to vacillate between obfuscation and moralism.) I discovered exactly three books—found neither in the school curriculums nor in the girl-lit tradition, but relegated to the netherworld of "Further Reading" appendixes.

The first, written by Karen Gravelle and her fifteen-year-old niece Jennifer Gravelle in 1996, is *The Period Book: Everything You Don't Want to Ask (But Need to Know)*. The book is short—110 pages—with lots of amusing illustrations. The Gravelles also give practical advice. If girls unexpectedly get their periods, they remind them that they can stuff toilet paper, paper towels, or even a sock in their underpants—and encourage them to ask other women for a pad, since "even total strangers will be perfectly happy to give you one." *The Period Book* is empowering even in subtle ways, giving girls permission to defy authority—"On occasion, you may be in class when you discover you've gotten your period . . . If, for some reason, the teacher refuses to excuse you from class, *get up and go anyway.*"[1] If a girl wonders, "What if I go to buy pads or tampons and the checkout clerk is a guy in my class?" they empower her to challenge convention "[One] way to deal with this is to decide that you're not going to let it embarrass you," the Gravelles write. "After all, most of the teenage and adult women in your town use these products, so chances are that this particular boy has probably already sold them to several girls that he knows."[2]

With some deftness, the Gravelles avoid the hollow hipness of teen magazines (where friends are "buds," boyfriends are "scopes" or "crushes," and guys who want sex are "booty hounds" or "stud puppies" conducting "scam-fests") without appearing to lecture from the other side of the divide. They even remind girls that they don't need special products for odors, helping them recognize manipulation when they see it:

You may also have noticed advertisements suggesting that women have to be particularly worried about "staying fresh" at certain times of the month. While they don't come right out and say it, they imply that a woman's vaginal area has an unpleasant odor when she's having her period . . . It just isn't the case.[3]

Best of all, the Gravelles talk about the conflicting feelings a girl has about getting her period for the first time. In a chapter titled "Is This Normal?" they answer a girl who observes, "Everyone else I know is dying to get their period, but I don't want it! Why can't I just stay the way I am?" by assuring her she can. "All the talk about how they are 'becoming a woman' may seem to mean that they can no longer do some of the things they've enjoyed up till now," the authors explain. "Or that they are supposed to become interested in other things—like makeup or boys—when they couldn't care less." In no uncertain terms, they reject this. "You don't have to change your feelings or your interests until you're ready!" they insist.[4]

In marked contrast to Molly (of 1950s *Molly Grows Up* fame), who sits forlornly beneath a tree twirling a dead leaf while the voice-over says, "Some of the things Molly used to do seem a little silly now," the Gravelles remind girls that "getting your period does not mean you have to become someone different." Next to this passage, they show a girl *in* a tree, clad in jeans, high-tops, and a baseball cap. "Remember, there are all different kinds of ways to be a woman. And you have plenty of time to figure out what kind of woman you want to be."[5]

A second book, *Sweet Secrets: Stories of Menstruation*, is the brainchild of Canadians Kathleen O'Grady and Paula Wansbrough. *Sweet Secrets* laces facts with short stories by various authors about girls having their first periods. The facts are straightforward. In explaining PMS, the authors remind girls that "not all women experience PMS although many may sometimes feel a few of the signs associated with PMS" and "not everyone can agree about what PMS is," admitting that "we also aren't sure what it's caused by."[6] They also dispel "menstrual myth number two" (menstrual myth number one is the you-can't-swim-when-you're-bleeding one), saying:

> Fact: Women can have sex when they have their periods. Some women may choose not to for various personal reasons while others really enjoy sex when they're bleeding . . . Remember also always to protect yourself from unwanted pregnancy and sexually transmitted diseases.[7]

Best of all, though, the short stories that form the bulk of *Sweet Secrets* give girls multiple perspectives on the event—from that of a girl who is flat on her back in a body cast when she gets her first period to that of a girl who has ten minutes between the national anthem and homeroom announcements to cope with her first period alone—so that *whatever* happens when the young reader gets hers, it falls within the spectrum of normal.

The best-known among the puberty authors is Lynda Madaras, who, true to tradition, wrote *The What's Happening to My Body? Book for Girls*, when her daughter entered puberty and Madaras discovered "there was no book for young girls on menstruation." She acknowledges that most girls are sensitive enough to pick up on the conflicting messages mothers send, saying "Menstruation Is a Wonderful Part of Being a Woman, a Unique Ability of Which You Should Be Proud," but hiding the evidence, whereas "none of us would think of hiding our toothbrushes under the sink or in the back corners of the bathroom cupboard."[8] Madaras suggests that parents explain to their daughters that when they were growing up, menstruation was considered "something unclean and unmentionable"; that this attitude is still with them on some level, so please excuse them if they act a little embarrassed.

Madaras has become a kind of spokesperson for puberty education, urging other educators and parents to shed the debilitating taboos surrounding menstruation. Her description of the menstrual cycle, while labored, is determinedly positive: "In a dream-like, slow-motion ballet, the tiny cilia caress the ripe ovum and gently move it along on its four-inch, four-day journey to the uterus."[9] Her book has a lot of practical advice, things I hadn't encountered elsewhere, like suggesting that a first-time tampon user try saliva or K-Y jelly on the applicator to facilitate insertion, or observing that "some women find masturbating to orgasm helpful" for relieving menstrual cramps.[10]

Unfortunately, while Madaras is quite sure archaic attitudes toward menstruation need to be corrected and is proactive on the subject, she backs away from a similar stance on sexuality. Here conventional moralism creeps in around the edges of good advice. The subtle message—girls ought to tie sex to emotional commitment or they'll be hurt—remains. (For example, if girls are weighing "French-kissing, petting, or going further," Madaras suggests that they ask themselves: "Will this person start rumors or gossip about you? Are you doing these things because you really care about this person or simply because you're curious to try these things?")[11] Worse, religious views about sex get equal play with progressive ones. Clearly,

Madaras has made a lot of concessions to make sure her book gets into school libraries, but by refusing to acknowledge that such attitudes toward sexuality can be just as repressive as those about menstruation, she undercuts her own efforts to de-mystify the topic.

THE MUSEUM: MONUMENT TO MENSTRUATION

Harry Finley, curator of the Museum of Menstruation, sets about the task of demystification in a different way. At first glance, his rec room is unremarkable. Vintage 1970s, it is plushly carpeted, wood-paneled, and features the requisite beanbag. Upon closer inspection, there are some peculiarities. Instead of the usual athletic trophies, diplomas, and macramé owls on the wall, there are tampons, sanitary pads, and mannequins modeling the latest menstrual fashions.

Welcome to MUM ("as in 'Mum's the word'), formally known as the Museum of Menstruation. Contents collected by, exhibit curated by, and tours given by Harry Finley. The museum, located in the basement of Finley's home in New Carrollton, Maryland, opened in August 1995, but Finley has been collecting menstrual paraphernalia for almost twenty years. Tall, soft-spoken, and eager to share his collection, Finley decided that a catamenial gallery with a historical perspective was the way to go. Living alone in his modest ranch house and thinking there was no reason his rec room couldn't serve multiple purposes—leisure plus hygienic lore—he drew on his legacy of "monuments to women" (Grandpa founded the Miss America contest) and dedicated his basement to the cause. It is certainly the D.C. area's strangest archival trove.

Finley has no feminist sensibility, no curator's sense of discrimination, no clever wryness about his subject. Yet with a hobbyist's devoted fervor, he has collected everything he could get his hands on, from patent-office diagrams of the original Rely tampon and German catalog descriptions of a "history of underwear" exhibit to an actual 1940s Modess pad still in its wrapper.

Opening the museum mostly on weekends and mostly by appointment, Finley says that, despite the fact that there's no sign announcing the museum's presence—he has no desire to invite zoning controversy or alert his fundamentalist Christian neighbors—he has had hundreds of word-of-mouth visitors.

Still, he's gotten some flak. As a federal government worker on orders from his employer not to reveal his specific association or, for that matter, to discuss his outside interest in menstrual products while on the job, Finley would reveal only that he works in a defense-related industry. (Once a colleague jokingly left a 3-D plaque on his desk, a tampon mounted like a model rocket and bearing the inscription "M1-TAMPON LAUNCHER.") When Finley invited one of his bosses to the museum opening, the man was shocked. "What if there's a police raid?" he asked. Finley was indignant. "My God, it's not pornography, it's menstruation!" He is genuinely perplexed by the reactions he gets.

Even the makers of menstrual products reject him; no representative from "the business" has ever dropped by to view Finley's collection. "The few times I've called anyone in the sanitary protection industry, there's mostly a lot of long pauses," Finley says sadly. He's surprised at their reticence and wonders why they don't share his enthusiasm for their products. In fact, they stonewall him. "It's like they're afraid to give away any secrets, like we're talking about nuclear arms or something!" When Finley had his museum opening and formally extended invitations to the folks at Kotex and Tambrands, among others, no one showed up. Only the Kotex execs bothered to respond, apologizing that they had a meeting that day. "On a Sunday!" Finley says with exasperation.

But then, Finley—pale, fastidious, and strangely earnest—is truly hard to get a handle on. Asked repeatedly in a dozen different ways why he finds menstrual artifacts so fascinating and why he has invested so much time and money in preserving them, Finley is vague, reluctant to dip into his psyche for the source of his obsession—or at least loath to share it with me. "It's just so interesting," he says with a shrug, and I get no more than that. Nothing in his home, or manner, or conversation, hints at an agenda. He seems genuine—though incongruously naive. As we sit alone in his cool basement, I have a recurring vision of Anthony Hopkins's solicitous Hannibal Lecter, and I keep reminding myself that my editor knows where I am. That my mom, a teacher, once had a colleague who had a potato museum in his house, so how weird is a menstrual museum? And that there's probably nothing significant in the fact that this knickknack-free house looks oddly temporary and totally unlived-in. So much so that when I don't see any signs of life in the bathroom—no hairs in the sink, no shampoo in the shower, no washcloth on the tub—I peek into the medicine cabinet and am duly chastised by a box of tampons with a note attached: "Hey! What did you expect? Help yourself. The management." However odd Finley's interest, this variation on come-over-and-look-at-my-rock-collection is so extraordinary it has to be sincere. And while I never convincingly locate the origins of this quiet, solitary man's interest in menstrual products, I'm delighted by his collection.

Finley has everything you ever wanted to know about menstruation—and then some. A skilled designer, he has created a massive Web site that makes much of his obscure collection available to the public. Today, almost every Web site or article that touches on menstruation ends with referrals and links to Finley's MUM site (www.mum.org).

Finley began collecting sanitary protection ads as a hobby, and today such ads form the bulk of his collection. He has foreign ads, contemporary ads, and historical ads. (Sometimes the contemporary ads hark back to the historical ones with products from the dark ages of sanitary protection. For example, in 1955 Sears offered special "Teen-Age Sanitary Garments" like the "new cotton puckerette Sanitary Panty." The santy panty, decorated with "bright, gay colors," featured a "moisture-resistant crotch which is rubber-lined." In 1997, Kotex advertised its brand-new Personals disposable "protective panties" by showing a girl pulling jeans on over her puckered-panties and promising, "You won't know how you managed without it.")

The MUM site also reprints articles from academic journals to fulfill its menstrual trivia mission. For example, Finley has embarked on a quest to discover whether animals such as sharks and bears are really attracted to the odor of menstrual fluid. Such tangents are entertaining—and occasionally surprising.

"Sound scientific documentation supporting such gender-biased malarkey is hard to find," he reports. "Actually, one is more likely to run across studies concluding quite the opposite." A 1991 article in the *Journal of Wildlife Management* reports the results of a series of U.S. Forest Service studies on the subject.

In one, used tampons were presented to foraging bears. If the bears ate the tampons, rolled on them, or sniffed them, researchers took that to mean they were attracted. In twenty out of twenty-two cases, the bears ignored the tampons. Two bears casually sniffed them. In another study, bears were offered a choice of unused tampons, tampons soaked in menstrual fluid, tampons soaked in human blood, and tampons soaked in rendered beef fat. (They were scattered along a walking path bears frequented.) Ten out of ten bears opted only for the rendered-beef-fat tampons. Then the Forest Service decided to experiment with live humans: eleven menstruating women wearing tampons and one menstruating woman who'd allowed blood to leak through her clothing. None of the ten bears the women encountered paid any attention. The study concluded with some up-close-and-personal encounters: "Another woman wearing external pads during two of her menstrual cycles hand-fed four female bears and walked within two meters of adult male bears during bear mating season and did not receive any attention."[12]

Next to such fairly reputable scientific studies, Finley displays commentary from Web-site visitors—some of it downright bizarre. Like the woman who wrote about her beagle Winchester's "uncanny ability to enter a room of up to 30 people (in an actual trial) and immediately identify a menstruating woman (by aggressively sniffing her)." The woman says she contacted two tampon manufacturers, offering Winchester's services to aid in their quest for the perfect deodorant tampon, and they rejected her offer. Indignant, she writes: "Kimberly-Clark maintains that most dogs will respond like Winchester! This is totally untrue, some dogs will sniff everybody's crotch randomly!"

Finley also attends the Society for Menstrual Cycle Research's biennial conventions and reports on the activities of both respected and maverick academics. He checks in on scientific theories like those of Margie Profet, who made headlines in 1993 by suggesting that menstruation's primary evolutionary function was to rid the uterus of bacteria, germs that hitchhiked their way into the uterus via sperm. Profet's theories have been widely criticized by biologists who say that blood gushing through an area doesn't necessarily clean it up, that the incidence of pelvic infection actually *increases* just after a menstrual period, and that bacteria arriving on the sperm that successfully fertilizes an egg—making the woman pregnant—would *not* be flushed out. Since until fairly recently, in evolutionary terms, women were either pregnant or nursing—and therefore not menstruating—during most of their adult lives, it doesn't make sense that menstruation would be a significant way of fighting disease.[13] (Profet's theory also echoes early ideas about menstrual blood bearing dangerous meat-spoiling-and-disease-causing toxins.)

Finley carefully chronicles debates like these, but rarely takes a stand on anything. He is a one-man movement, persuaded that the sheer quantity of his "stuff" will lend legitimacy to his cause, even if we never actually learn what his cause is. His politics are never clear. In one brochure for the museum, he writes, "Men are basically excluded from the world of menstruation—except as the target of a PMS mood, or the recipient of a time-of-month explanation for not having sex. For women (and *men!*), menstruation is a messy, smelly, unpredictable and—*yuk!*—*bloody* nuisance."

POWER IN THE BLOOD

My Blood, my blood,
My Blood's a flood.
My Blood's a raging sea,
My Blood's a hundred hissing cats
Communing inside of me.

This Blood it honors our creation
To bring life into gestation.
It joins us with the Moon, the Sea,
Sisters of Powers that be . . .
—Shana Grace (www.yOni.com)

Surfing the Net, browsing "womyn's" magazines, and perusing contemporary feminist literature, I discover a collection of women determined to resist the prevailing culture of secrecy and shame surrounding menstruation. They offer a bizarre kind of resistance—one that reads almost as retreat.

I call them the Celebrate-Your-Cycles feminists. They're goddess-feminists with a 1990s twist, and their philosophy goes something like this: Womyn's periods, being cyclical in nature, allow them to more readily commune with the earth, moon, and tide cycles—and being closer to nature, they're naturally more nurturing. We should celebrate and cultivate these spiritual connections. Hip, hip, hooray, menstruation! Let's collect our bloody effluent and return it to the earth, or at least water our houseplants with it. ("Go to a field, a wood, somewhere and bleed on the earth: share with her and feel what happens," Jennifer Stonier urged Society for Menstrual Cycle Research conventiongoers in 1995.[14]) Another *recycler* suggests soaking used cloth pads in the "moon bowl" she offers for a modest price and using this "rich soaking water" on gardens and plants for "amazing results.")

Surf the Net and the Celebrate-Your-Cyclists are almost everywhere periods pop up (except in the sites generated by the sanitary protection industry, of course). One Web 'zine called yOni (www.yOni.com)—*yoni* is a term for women's genitals—describes itself as a "celebration of the feminine." The yOni authors explain that "women are cyclic creatures, rising and ebbing to the tune of the Moon and the flow of the waters." Riffing on this theme in the Moon Hutch Web site's article titled "Anthropological and Historical Notes on Menstruation," Jean Tracy describes menstruation as "fertile fuel for life on earth," insisting that it represents "abundance and creativity." To take full advantage of the moon-womb link—as the goddess-feminists argue primitive women did—menstruaters should synchronize their cycles with the moon so that a full moon coincides with ovulation. In case there are skeptics out there, Tracy offers scientific proof: "This summer, I had the opportunity to test this theory," she writes. "I slept out on the porch with the light of the Full Moon gracing my body the entire night. Indeed, I did ovulate the next day and consequently started my menses one week early on the dark of the moon." Sadly, the synchronization lasted only one cycle. "This could be due to the fact that I slept indoors and utilized artificial light the rest of the month," Tracy speculates. She hopes that one day, "through genetic memory, we might reclaim a time when the feminine cycle was integrated into our common experience of life."

The Celebrate-Your-Cyclists romanticize matriarchies by suggesting they were once pervasive across cultures and continents and by inaccurately situating them on a linear map of history where they predate all patriarchies. These female chieftains were a kinder, gentler breed of women, who were in touch with their bodies. The Cyclists yearn for a return to that era. To get back in touch with their "wise-womyn" ways, many Celebrate-Your-Cyclists urge a new set of rituals involving moon calendars (charting and properly synchronizing menstrual cycles with the moon), initiation rites (replete with workshops where adolescent girls can construct "menstrual crowns" and plan "period parties" for their menstrual coming-out), and seclusion rites (a miniretreat designed to make "a spiritual connection between a woman's body and the moon, between the act of creation and her existence as a woman").

Such groups sing the praises of menstrual huts, places where bleeding women go once a month to get away from men, to relax, to unwind, to drink herbal teas, and to let their blood flow out onto cushy moss carpets. On the Wombcycle for Women site (www.moon-myst.com), "Cyber-nana" explains that "the responsibility for establishing a healthy next generation requires that we honor our young women[,] for they are the vessels in which the new generation begins." To that end, she rhapsodizes about the ancient "moonlodge" practice. "This was a time for women to gather and take time to praise the goddess that is within them," she writes. "While in the solitude of the moonlodge, they would be inspired to create a gift for the family, maybe a new way to prepare venison or a new design for blanket weaving."

Modern anthropologists have indeed documented the existence of menstrual huts in various tribes, from Suriname to Canada's Northwest Territories. But while the goddess-feminists hype the concept by implying that the isolation is a consensual, affirmative process, others argue, more persuasively, that such practices—even in modern manifestations such as the *mikvah*, a ritual bath for Orthodox Jews, and *niddah*, a period when Orthodox Jewish women who are menstruating are not allowed any physical contact with their spouses—are pollution taboos. That is, women are perceived as contaminated and are barred from public life.

For the most part, modern proponents of menstrual huts propose diluted forms of these practices, more self-help than communal ritual. These activities are designed to help women realize that bleeding is "a time of power, where we can gather our wisdom by taking time out to go within," according to Tracy. The recommendations include everything from sipping a glass of wine in a relaxing bath to taking time out on those special days to free-associate with refrigerator-poem magnets. This interpretation of a woman's menstrual cycles as a time for her to commune with her inner source of power dates back to the rise of cultural feminism in the late 1970s. In 1978 British authors Penelope Shuttle and Peter Redgrove published *The Wise Wound: The Myths, Realities, and Meanings of Menstruation*, which romanticized menstruation as a source of women's spiritual power. Shuttle and Redgrove borrowed smatterings of history, religion, and literature to argue that the ancients understood the transformative nature of menstruation, recognized it as a source of women's power, and cultivated and celebrated it. We should do the same, they argued. One scenario, touted as ideal, presents a new world order where birth would be a "triple-blood" event. The midwife would be menstruating; the mother, of course, would bleed giving birth; and the placenta, which "is like a twin brother or sister in the womb," would emerge covered in blood and be "killed to give us life," dying for us "like Jesus on the Cross."[15] All of the reverence for blood is designed to help women get in touch with their ancient spiritual powers.

The authors use an old tactic, the idealization of womanhood, but with a twist. Woman's gentle and nurturing nature has long been based on her role as Mother. Shuttle and Redgrove push the parameters backwards, saying that it's *menstruation* and a woman's life-giving *potential* that imbue her with this greater wisdom. They urge women to access their "menstrual energy" by meditating on the "Menstrual Mandala." (As far as I could make out, the Menstrual Mandala was a cross-shaped image with menstruation and ovulation at top and bottom—premenstruation and preovulation form the cross-bar tips—which women are supposed to mentally link, like the "God's-eye" cross you wove with yarn in the craft tent at Scout camp.) When women were in touch with their "feminine knowledge," the world would be a better place. "Women know naturally how precious life-in-the-body is," they explain. "Such care cannot make atomic bombs . . . Make food of love, not war."[16]

It would be easy to dismiss such texts, steeped as they are in quaint 1970s rhetoric, were their legacy not still around. While readership of *The Wise Wound* was surely limited, the trickle-down effects of such thinking endure—on all the aforementioned Web sites and in all the goddess-feminist books that proliferate today. And such reasoning has been a persistent strand in feminism for a hundred years, from the time of the suffragettes, who based their right to the franchise on their moral superiority over men, to contemporary eco-feminists and peace-feminists who premise their arguments on women's closeness to nature and inherent gentle pacifism. This kind of feminism, dubbed "cultural feminism" by scholars, colors the language of most mainstream discourse on women's rights. It is problematic on many levels. By accepting most of the cultural stereotypes about woman's innate nature, it narrows rather than broadens the realm of what is acceptable. Women are still defined oppositionally to men, but they're reminded to be proud of these differences. ("Whether as mothers, sisters, lovers, friends . . . womyn are priestesses of the heart and hearth, bearers of families, creators of culture," enthuses "Masawa, Crone Consultant," in the introduction to the booklet We'Moon '98.) Hoping to convert restrictive gender roles from liabilities into assets, this brand of feminism deifies women as goddesses. Likewise, the Celebrate-Your-Cyclists practice a brand of feel-good feminism that turns the fight away from outward sources (a determinedly sexist society) to inward ones (get in touch with your feminine nature and you'll feel a lot better), favoring inner reflection over activism. They argue, not that organized religion is an oppressive force, but rather that prevailing religious *interpretations* are oppressive. For them, it's a simple case of personal transformation. It's all in how you think about it. As Shuttle and Redgrove muse: "When is a Curse not a Curse? . . . When it's a blessing in disguise."[17]

BIRTH OF A NEW MENSTRUAL PRODUCT:
INSYNC MINIFORMS

*Your body is a ship of discovery. It carries you from girlhood to
womanhood. From having a mother to maybe being a mother.
It takes you far from your beginnings, and it never allows you to
go back. And every month along the way, it marks the journey.*
—inSync Miniforms ad, 1997

In a suburb south of Portland, Oregon, in a nondescript industrial park, a brand-new menstrual product is being born.
Called inSync Miniforms, this pad-tampon hybrid is designed
for "women's light days." It's the size and shape of a flattened
tampon, but soft, like a pad. Describing the product to investors and the media, company spokespeople like to cradle it
between two fingers, lengthwise, and explain that "it is held in
place naturally, by a woman's own anatomy." What they mean
is, a woman's labia, or vaginal lips, keep the miniform in place.

It's a fairly effective product. I am wearing one at the moment—day three of my menstrual cycle—and it works just fine
for those tapering-flow days. No better, no worse than a panty
liner.

But inSync is radically new in one respect: packaging. Because the miniform and the company that makes it, A-Fem, are
newcomers to sanitary protection, they have a remarkable
opportunity. They can start from scratch. In January of 1999,
inSync will have its national rollout. As preparation, the company is sending the product to stores and developing a marketing campaign to support it in the Pacific Northwest. The

planning stage serves as an instructive case study. How does a new menstrual product arrive on the market when consumers—real women—are consulted about its presentation? Women told company representatives that they were tired of pastel butterflies and ballerinas. And A-Fem, a tiny start-up company operating without the weight of history, listened.

In the sanitary protection aisles, inSync stands out. There, feminine hygiene etiquette is writ in blood; few deviate. It's a world where underpants are always "panties," where cum is "discharge," and where blood is always "fluid" (and usually blue). Once in a while, manufacturers venture out on a poetic limb. "Only Playtex has a double-layer design that gently blooms to fit the contours of your body," the company says on its Silk Glides package, depicting the tampon as a rose (dangling string serves as stem) and skillfully skirting all mention of placement. No one ever puts anything up their vaginas; tampons are *worn internally*. Women don't *bleed*, they *flow*. And, in what is perhaps the oddest concession to modesty, the word *menstruation* never appears on a single package. Anywhere.

Nestled in among the pale blues and pinks, inSync sticks out like a pariah among pads. Packaged in earth tones, inSync boldly instructs women to place the miniform between "the labia." On the back of the box there are no cartoon illustrations; no sketches of flying, winged pads; and no yellow roses. Instead, there is a *photograph* of the product. The words *menstrual flow* actually appear on the box. The inSync ads speak boldly. "Every month you have a period," the copy says. "It is not something that needs to be covered up, danced around or deodorized."

A-Fem is banking on the demise of menstrual modesty. The marketing department hopes that it's interpreting the focus-group data correctly. A-Fem's survival probably hinges on it. And yet, in some ways, the company has no choice but to adopt a forward-looking policy. When A-Fem tried to launch the product according to the old rules of menstrual marketing, it was a disaster.

In the beginning there was Fresh 'n' Fit Padettes. The padette (miniform) was invented by a physician at a hospital in New York whose wife, an avid tennis player, had stress incontinence (i.e., when she sneezed or laughed or coughed, she'd have some urine leakage). Pads were cumbersome for sports, and tampons didn't work for her problem. The doctor fooled around with various materials and shapes and came up with a small, absorbent rayon pad that was held in place by a woman's vaginal lips. His wife—so A-Fem company lore goes—loved this little "padette."

The product was christened the Fresh 'n' Fit Padette and tucked into a pastel package bearing a floral design. It was introduced to consumers in Tallahassee, Florida, in 1989, then withdrawn, and reintroduced in 1996, when A-Fem mailed 300,000 free samples to Tallahasee residents, addressed to "the woman of the house." The response was lukewarm. Those who used the product seemed to like it, but new customers were slow in coming.

Instead of spending heavily on mass-market ads, the mostly male CEOs at A-Fem decided to invest in a campaign to educate gynecologists and nurses about the padette. But since most women visit their gynecologists only once a year and rarely discuss menstrual products with them, this was a slow, laborious, and ultimately ineffective approach.

In 1996, Sarah Van Dyck joined A-Fem as director of marketing and sales. A young woman with impressive credentials from Proctor & Gamble, Van Dyck was articulate and aggressive—and she was persuaded that something was very, very wrong with the marketing plan for Fresh 'n' Fit. She urged the CEOs to pull the product, which had had marginal sales in Florida anyway, and to reconsider its presentation. She thought A-Fem needed to do some serious market research and possibly rethink the product. The name, the floral-and-pastel packaging, the advertising campaign—all seemed off-base to her. She approached the board. "This product needs a new name if it's going to sell," she insisted. But board members were reluctant to rename it, worrying about the vast inventory they had—hundreds of thousands of padettes, all labeled Fresh 'n' Fit. Van Dyck persisted, and a compromise was reached. The company would put production and marketing of Fresh 'n' Fit on hold while Van Dyck commissioned the requisite marketing research; if the numbers backed up her instincts, the padette name and image would be completely retooled.

———

At 10 a.m. on a Saturday morning in Seattle, ten women file into a conference room, agreeing to exchange their opinions on menstrual products for $50 apiece. The focus group does not know that the client is A-Fem, but only that they are there to talk about periods. A woman in her mid-thirties, Leah Knight, serves as A-Fem's moderator and moves the women from one topic to another, and through a series of exercises, with swift efficiency. She begins by having the women introduce themselves,* then explains the rules of the game: the women are being videotaped; they are being observed from behind a two-way mirror; they should feel free to disagree with one another; they are to be completely frank.

The women seem slightly ill at ease—but pleased that someone thinks their opinion is worthwhile—and quickly enter into the spirit of things. The conversation unfolds like a menstrual consciousness-raising group. The women arrive without having given sanitary protection much thought. Asked to consider the meaning and message of sanitary protection ads, they're annoyed. They kvetch. They grow indignant. All of them speak at once.

"We don't usually talk about it that way."

"Not in those terms."

"All those euphemisms."

Diane, a child-care worker in her late twenties, gains the floor. "The words themselves, *feminine protection*, amuse me," she says. "We all know what we're talking about, so why not just say it?"

The women wonder why no one will come right out and say "periods."

Tanya, a massage therapist and artist in her mid-thirties, has a theory. "It's probably some man that came up with using that [in ads] because he couldn't bring himself to say the words."

---

*I have changed their names.

"Definitely there's nothing positive about it in commercials," says Nora, a young woman who works in a bank. She is silent for a moment, trying to sort out just what she means. "It's like they're saying we need all that stuff just to make us better."

"Like those ads for douches!" Tanya says.

"Yeah, like those conversations they have, where they're like, 'Mom, I'm not feeling fresh.' *Fresh*, what's that about?" Diane says.

"Or those panty liners with scents," Nora adds. "All this stuff like we're gross. I don't particularly . . . well, I don't like that."

All around the table, women nod their heads in assent. As the session progresses, the women get freer about laying out their pet peeves. How come ads hardly ever show what the product looks like? How come they never say how many come in a box? How come these things cost so much? How come there is so much unnecessary packaging (pads separately wrapped in plastic inside a box sealed with plastic)? How come the women in the ads always look so pulled-together and always wear white—"Who wears white when they're bleeding?" Most of all, though, the women want to know why advertisers always go for "cute."

"Cutesy ads are offensive," says Diane, the plump child-care worker who is emerging as a leader in the fast-paced dynamics of the focus group. She is articulate, and summarizes for the other women. "When you try to cutesy it up, it's like you're saying the real thing is so unpalatable you can't even speak about it. You have to hide it and make it all pretty."

"Yeah," Elaine, an engineer, agrees. "It's like they're saying it's a gross topic we're going to talk about, so we're going to dance around it."

"Instead of saying, 'This is an everyday happening,'" Tanya interjects, "'and we're going to talk about it in practical terms.'"

A-Fem, makers of inSync, took these words to heart. Working with the Seattle-based advertising firm of Herring/Newman, the marketing department came up with a new mandate. The company would boldly go where no maker of menstrual products had gone before: to the uncharted territory of nonchalance.

"Every month you have a period. You do not have a problem or an illness," inSync's signature ad would read. "Life does not come to a halt because of it. You do not need to be protected from it. It happens because it needs to. It's that simple." The ad features a black-and-white photo of a thirty-something woman. She wears jeans, a sweater, clogs—none of which are white. A photograph of the product appears.

The other two ads in the miniform print campaign are also a striking departure, not so much because of what they say, but because of who says it. One features a very young girl, maybe twelve. This inSync Girl is not lying on a bed in her girlish teenage bedroom, feet crossed at the ankles and talking on the phone (Tampax ad). She is not hiding from the gym teacher in a locker because her P.E. uniform is white and she might bleed through (Always ad). And she is not fretting about "accidents" or seeking reassurance that "no one ever has to know you have your period" (Stayfree Ultra Thin ad). The inSync Girl is about the age most girls actually are when they get their first period. Her hair is uncombed and she doesn't seem to care, or even notice. She doesn't appear to be wearing makeup. She wears round, owlish glasses, and she lies on the grass, presumably thinking.

In the third ad in this series, the model wears Doc Martens, jeans, a work shirt, funky earrings. Her long hair is caught in a barrette, and she is striking—though not conventionally pretty—in a chiseled, Georgia O'Keefe kind of way. She is fiftyish; she has wrinkles.

This Georgia O'Keefe woman came out of a list of adjectives the focus group selected. Given a couple of dozen words to rank, words that would describe the ideal feminine-protection role model, the group chose *confident, straightforward, smart, healthy, strong, fit, individual.* They rejected *shy, delicate, conventional, modest,* and *proper.* In the course of imagining a new kind of sanitary protection ad, the advertisers put together a video that personified the messages they were getting.

The words "Decade 1990s" flash on the screen. Des'ree belts out the lyrics to *You Gotta Be* as Thelma and Louise fly over a cliff, Tina Turner grinds her hips, Jackie Kennedy waves to a crowd, Lucille Ball gives her impish smile, Bonnie Raitt croons, Mother Teresa feeds the poor, Hillary Rodham Clinton speaks to the nation, Ellen DeGeneres is her out-and-proud self. Girls are rowing boats, women are fishing, demonstrators are marching for equal rights for all, while Des'ree hammers on that "you gotta be" strong and bold.

This is inSync's wet dream. This is the advertising spot A-Fem *would* broadcast if they had the big, big bucks to exhibit this collection of spokespeople in a fantasy world where these celebrities would, for a moment, consider representing a sanitary protection company.

But by the time A-Fem advertising agency Herring/Newman settles down to produce the real TV spot—relegating this rough cut to investor meetings and sales rallies—they've toned things down somewhat. Still, the finished product remains provocative.

Created by Charlotte Moore, the art director responsible for the trend-setting multipage Nike ads—such as the one that begins with the question "Did you ever wish you were a boy?"—these ads aired first in the Pacific Northwest, where people are known for being slightly liberal, slightly funky, slightly more likely to try a new product. A-Fem introduced inSync there in January 1998.

The spot opens with a little girl on her tiptoes, struggling to see above the counter and into the mirror in a public restroom. A parade of women follows, each pausing to study her reflection. The commercial is in color, but has the gritty, black-and-white feel of a documentary. The women—girls, teens, older women, young women, black women, white women—do not look like models. They are normal-looking women, shot Dorothea Lange–style to look heroic. As they pass through the women's room, examining themselves in the mirror, type runs across the screen: "She is . . . oblivious, proud, thinking, embarrassed, thankful, certain." The voice-over introduces us to "inSync Miniforms, a whole new choice in feminine protection."

Life as a startup in the menstrual products industry can be tough. But A-Fem is determinedly optimistic. As one of the company's videos, intended for prospective investors, observes, "There are 898 shampoos, 340 wrinkle creams, 1752 shades of red lipstick, 12,031 diet plans, and two forms of feminine protection."

What the video doesn't say is that these two forms of feminine protection—made by three corporate giants—control 98 percent of the sanitary protection market. Will these big guys allow an incursion by A-Fem, a spunky little company that's looking to change the rules of the game? (A-Fem president Peter Burke admitted that this was the biggest concern potential investors voiced.) Procter & Gamble originally worried enough to option certain padette technical and marketing rights for $2 million in April of 1997. But a year later, P&G let the option expire, confident—especially with its new Tambrands acquisition—that A-Fem had nothing it wanted and posed no serious threat. After all they're not exactly in the same league.

When I visit A-Fem early one December morning, Sarah Van Dyck hustles me across the industrial park, from the corporate headquarters on one side of the parking lot to the manufacturing plant on the other. We are rushing to see the factory in action.

Clearly, the assembly line has been revved up for my benefit. The small, cement-floored room contains exactly three factory workers. Sort of. Actually, the solitary production line is being staffed by the company's regulatory affairs director, its quality-control engineer, and its chief—and only—mechanic. It is usually staffed by temp workers, Van Dyck explains, but all of them, inexplicably, called in sick today. No matter. "This is a company where everybody pitches in and does what they can," Van Dyck explains.

Dressed in white smocks and pale-blue hair nets, the three department heads feed a pliable rope of rayon into a machine that sews a channel along the top, encloses it in polypropylene webbing (the better to wick moisture from the surface), and chops it to Vienna-sausage size. Each rayon weenie is then enveloped in the corporate logo, sealed in a paper wrapper, and shot out from a conveyor belt. Someday soon the company hopes to have an "electronic eye" at the end of its assembly line. The eye will know if two miniforms were accidentally squeezed into one wrapper or if an empty wrapper is slipping by. In the interim, Pat Feetham, director of regulatory affairs for the company, is acting as quality controller.

She snatches an "empty" off the conveyor belt and tosses it into a trash can. "We also do a culture with each batch of finished products to make sure there are no bugs with the production process," Feetham says, explaining that they will check the sample for correct size and placement of stitching as well as test the material to make sure no metal shards from the machinery—or anything else—land in the miniform. She grabs three "mistakes" off the line, then two more, sending them sailing toward the trash. "And we're one of the only sanitary protection manufacturers to do that. Most do quality controls only in the beginning, not with the finished product."

Moments later, something gets jumbled in one of the machines and the whole line stops. Feetham takes the time to explain her reasoning behind the random-sampling quality-control checks: "Until we have lots and lots of history, we have to be super-sure of the quality of our product."

I watch as they fiddle around with the machine, trying to remove whatever has obstructed their assembly line. The plant manager teases a recalcitrant puff of rayon from between wedges of metal. He flicks a switch and the machines roar to life again. Everyone gets back to work.

It is regular and repetitive and dull work. Because the machines aren't encased in plastic, each event in the life cycle of the miniform is visible. All the mystery behind the product's formulation and its ultimate use is eliminated here under the fluorescent lights of the factory floor.

"That's all there is to it," Sarah Van Dyck says with a shrug as we exit.

The inSync marketing campaign is dedicated to openness. "Research strongly points to the conclusion that the time is here for a new style of advertising for feminine protection," Leah Knight, the focus-group moderator, points out. That said, she adds a few caveats. After all, A-Fem researchers discovered that women *claimed* they wanted straight-talking ads, but actually qualified that with a lot of talk about "appropriateness."

Folding the results of the earlier focus group in with those of three others, and combining them with hundreds of short interviews conducted with women at malls, Knight wrote up her survey results for A-Fem. The conclusions, compiled in a 1996 report called "Attitudes Toward Feminine Protection and Perceptions Toward Fresh 'n' Fit," sounds eerily similar to the Tampax report issued some fifteen years ago. "Even in today's world, women still seem to have some level of discomfort associated with discussing feminine protection products and menstruation," Knight concludes in her report. She observes that most women today don't talk about menstruation in front of men. "Even those with spouses seemed hesitant to discuss the subject with their significant other," she says, noting that most women said they "would never send their husbands to the grocery store to purchase feminine protection products, usually because they felt their husband would be embarrassed." Though women were annoyed at the euphemisms and sense of secrecy in ads for menstrual products, they continued to worry about ads that were so frank as to be offensive. When Knight threw out several statements—"*Menstruation* is not a bad word" and "It's time women talked more openly about their periods"—there was disagreement. For some, *menstruation* was a bad word. Many disagreed that women should speak more openly about their periods. They continued to emphasize that they liked products that allowed them be especially "discreet" about their periods.

They insisted that ads should maintain a "level of appropriateness and respect," specifying that humorous ads were "in bad taste." The women felt certain venues—such as women's magazines—were okay for detailed discussions of menstruation, but that TV spots, especially ones airing during the prime-time hours they spent watching TV with their husbands, should make only veiled references to what the product was used for. The inSync TV spot straddles the line perfectly: it is a feel-good ad about womanhood that creates product awareness without ever mentioning the words *menstruation*, *periods*, *blood*, *leakage*, or *placement*. And indeed, most current TV advertising guidelines demand such vagueness, insisting, as NBC does, that ads for menstrual products meet "the stringent standards of good taste" by modest references to "grooming," "freshness," and "femininity" and discouraging, in most cases, the inclusion of men or children in the ads. There are also rules, which vary from affiliate to affiliate, specifying when such ads can air—usually not in prime time—and honoring the wishes of various producers, like Disney, who forbid feminine hygiene commercials during their programs. While there are probably plenty of ten-, eleven-, and twelve-year-old girls watching *The Wonderful World of Disney*, the corporation is clearly sensitive to parents' wishes, sparing them the awkward unpleasantness of explaining menstruation to their youngsters.

The restrictions placed on sanitary protection commercials by a conservative company like Disney are hardly surprising. What is startling is to see how the assumption that menstruation is something we simply don't talk about in public persists, even among liberal, well-educated middle-class women—the Seattle focus group being a case in point.

As the focus group's discussion continues, it becomes clear just how conflicted women today still are about menstruation. They're indignant that advertisers act as though menstruation were an embarrassment that had to be danced around, and yet the subject is embarrassing enough that they warn advertisers to be "careful" and not to "offend" anybody by talking about it "inappropriately." The consciousness-raising of the focus group only goes so far. The observations never make the leap into analysis. And why should they? This is a focus group, after all, sponsored by a menstrual products company. What inSync discovers is that women still feel remarkably ambivalent about their periods. And not ambivalence of the it's-a-drag-to-get-cramps-and-pimples variety, but ambivalence about how open people should be about the topic. For Beth, a health-care administrator, anxiety creeps in around the edges of what she is saying. For example, it's *embarrassing* when a tampon ad runs on TV and there might be guys in the room with you. "I'm more likely to pay attention to an ad [like this] when it's in a magazine rather than on TV, because I have the freedom to look at it or not, and to know it's not offending anybody."

Tanya, the massage therapist, agrees. "I wish there were a way to disseminate that kind of information without embarrassing one half of the population."

"Well, what words do you use to talk about this?" Leah, the moderator, interjects. It turns out many of the women still use code words—just different code words.

"I think you say, 'I'm PMS,'" offers Nora, the woman who works in a bank.

Tanya takes the you've-come-a-long-way-baby line: "Our generation doesn't really have the stigma of talking about it, like, 'My red aunt has come.'" The group laughs. "It's more like, 'I have cramps' or 'I have PMS.' The euphemisms are much closer to the topic . . . if you can still call them that."

Leah is intrigued. "But do you talk about it differently with women than with men?"

There is a chorus of no's. But the denials seem odd in the face of what follows.

"I don't really talk about it to men," explains Lynn, who works in a bookstore.

"You can say, 'I have cramps,' but they don't really get it," Nora explains.

"The only male I talk about it to is my spouse," says Lisa, a graduate student. She goes on to describe what offends *him* in the ads.

The women also express resentment and confusion around the scent issue—what *I think* as opposed to what *they say* women's experiences are. Each one relies on personal experience to say she doesn't even notice an odor, or has never thought hers a bad odor, or has never worried about odor. But they lack the confidence to say, This isn't accurate, and instead say, That's not me.

"Well, maybe for some people smell is a problem," Beth says. "Well, some people are plagued with that problem, but I never have been. Smell, I don't know . . ."

Diane, the child-care worker, is more bluntly dismissive. "I think it's an issue that gets raised a lot, but it's not really a problem for me. I remember, when I was young, someone telling me it's going to smell bad . . ."

". . . and it didn't!" Lisa says, finishing her sentence for her. None of them know women for whom this is a problem, but since they don't really talk about it with most of their friends, they accept the advertisers' contention that smell is a problem for *some*—maybe even *most*—women.

Later, when the moderator presents the women with a statement—"My period is a fact of life and I have a sense of humor about it"—it becomes obvious that some of the women continue to feel that the subject of menstruation should still be treated with kid gloves. Joking about bleeding would be akin to walking through a minefield: there are all kinds of dangers. While they have trouble articulating why this kind of humor is problematic, they imply that these would be "dirty" jokes.

"The idea's a little offensive," Laurie, a stay-at-home mom, says. "I don't want an ad—some pad ad—that's funny. I don't want to laugh."

"But jokes on the wrapper would be good!" Lynn teases.

"A funny ad would be a very fine line to walk without offending people," asserts Diane.

But Lynn refuses to dismiss the idea completely. You would

just have to be "careful." She gets into the spirit of things by proposing the kind of ad that might finesse these concerns. It's a revealing scenario. "Like I'm thinking, what if I planned my tenth wedding anniversary in Hawaii and the day you arrive, you're getting ready to put on your little bikini and you find out you've got your period. I mean, you would have to laugh about it. And you'd have to find other things to do than maybe celebrating the way you'd planned to."

The women nod in agreement and the conversation takes a different turn. But I keep returning to this comment, struck by her implications. What activities would Lynn shy away from, and why? Why does bleeding preclude bikini-wearing? Is she too worried about leakage to be comfortable with a tampon alone? And by referring to other ways of "celebrating," is she implying she wouldn't have sex while menstruating? (According to the Tampax study, the belief that women should not have sex while menstruating is shared by more than half the country. While having sex during menstruation is an admittedly messy affair and people may prefer not to do it, it's still astonishing that so many people assume it *should not* be done. If Lynn is *not* talking about sex, then what activities would she be restricted from? Her period is not simply an inconvenience—Oh, now I have to bring a fanny pack when I hike the Waianae Mountains—it means there are certain things she would not do. Whatever the scope of her changes in plans, her period requires her to adjust her thinking and behavior, setting her outside the norms of everyday life. It was an off-the-cuff comment, but a telling one.

In 1981, the Tampax report suggested that 30 percent of all Americans believed women needed to restrict their activities when menstruating. As Lynn's comments—and the "yeah's" of assent that rippled through the group—indicate, that belief is alive and well today.

Typically, one woman said that bleeding is "not something that bothers me, it's a natural thing," but referred to leaking as "social suicide."

When push came to shove, the ad agency and its client listened to the most cautious. "I kinda feel like none of this specific stuff should be in TV ads," one woman said. "I don't want to see the product. I don't want to talk about blood. I don't want any of it."

"So you want enough to create awareness but nothing specific about the product at all?" Leah asks.

"Yeah."

The agency and A-Fem listened to this voice, and all the concerns about "appropriateness" and "inoffensiveness" and "embarrassment," and tailored its TV commercial accordingly. A basically conservative industry designed to pick up on subtle anxieties, sanitary protection companies are masters at manipulating and reflecting these anxieties back. No matter what inSync may profess to believe about a new openness, its ads reflect women's views right back at them. In the finest Feminism Lite tradition, the copy for inSync's TV commercial would make you feel good about being a woman without making the slightest allusion to why you might have been feeling bad in the first place. As the women parade through the public rest room in the TV spot, a voice-over tells us, "A woman spends her entire life responding to her changing body. Dealing with her monthly cycle is just another way to practice." No products pictured. No explanations necessary. No possible way to offend—or enlighten—anyone. Perfect.

Conclusion

T wenty years after writing out my theorems and postulates in a small blue Mead memo notebook, I feel a little as if I am rehashing the same issues—this time in a big red notebook called *The Curse*. I am still hoping that if I arrange and itemize things with the if-then logic of geometry, my lines of inquiry will resolve themselves into tidy, irrefutable corners. But my theorems and postulates read like riddles rather than revelations. Menstruation is taught in schools because it's "natural," but treated as though it's nasty. Menstruation is normal, but the attendant hormonal flux is a disease. Menstruation is obsessively hidden, yet its real disappearance—menopause—engenders disdain. Menstruation doesn't *really* have anything to do with sexuality, yet it shares all its taboos.

After spending almost two years doing nothing but reading and thinking about periods, I continue to find menstrual etiquette perplexing. Why has this elaborate system of subterfuge evolved—and, more important, endured? The answers I come up with are vague and amorphous. It is easier to say what I *don't* think.

I don't think it's a conspiracy generated by a small coven of advertising and industry executives—though I think they've capitalized on and exploited our phobias. I don't think euphemisms like "the curse" have evolved simply because bleeding is inconvenient and we get cramps. And I don't think "tradition" or religious doctrine accounts entirely for our behavior (at least, I don't think it is the interesting part of the answer, the bit that gets us closer to understanding why we continue to respect these customs).

On the other hand, I *do* think our menstrual etiquette persists because it shores up a slew of problematic beliefs about women and reproduction, sex, sexuality, and power. Menstruation belongs in the swelling heap of feminist thought, the pile labeled "Women's Bodies Are a Battleground," as it is yet another example of our culture's troubling propensity to project a host of anxieties onto women's bodies. These "projections" are debilitating because they distort our reality. They color our perceptions and inform our behavior.

In the course of writing this book, I've become aware of the way I self-censor conversations about my work. When women ask me what I'm up to these days, I tell them I'm working on a book about menstruation and the culture of concealment surrounding it. I chat on about the advertising, the sex-ed tracts, the teen magazines, toxic shock and dioxin. When men ask me the same question, I tell them I'm writing a book. If they pursue the matter, I tell them that I'm working on a book about menstruation—*never* "periods," because menstruation at least sounds slightly clinical and scientific and weighty. I talk to them about the sanitary protection industry and dioxin and TSS for the same reasons. I assume that health issues lend credence to what might otherwise be dismissed as frivolous. I shy away from, or rush through, the rest of my thesis, believing that these men would find it uninteresting—or worse, embarrassing—to discuss. Sometimes I catch myself—"How can you be writing a book about the hush surrounding menstruation and then perpetuate it?"—and make myself frankly describe my book. But the act requires a conscious effort.

I have puzzled over this behavior. Why do I act this way? And what difference does it make?

The "why" comes easier. I do this because I am hyperaware of periods as a "girl thing." To talk openly with men about bleeding seems strange. Doing so makes me feel weird. Despite the fact that a quarter of us women in our reproductive years are menstruating at any given time, it feels *abnormal* to acknowledge this to men.

What difference does my reticence—quite typical, I believe—make? It matters because as long as *not* menstruating is perceived as the norm—and why else would we hide it?—women will always be the Other. Hushing up the fact of menstruation facilitates the illusion that it's not happening. Non-bleeding becomes a standard from which all others deviate. Women are left wondering what it is about this experience that renders it inappropriate for public discussion. Where is my reality? And how does the knowledge that our reality is "inappropriate" affect our faith in our perceptions and the sense of entitlement that comes from trusting that our experience is representative? How does living on the margins, as the Other, affect us?

After a while it becomes psychologically disorienting for women to look out at a world where their reality doesn't exist. Menstruation itself does not create this effect, but it dovetails nicely with all the other images and myths about bodies, sexuality, and desire that women encounter—ideas that are more proscriptive than enlightening.

For example, feminists have frequently railed against the narrow sexual paradigms our culture offers up to women—Madonna (saint and mother) or Eve (slut and temptress). In a 1980 essay in *Signs: Journal of Women in Culture and Society*, feminist Elizabeth Janeway asserts that these masculine archetypes of female sexuality are "attempts to manipulate woman's vision of herself" and that "coming out of an alien understanding, as they do, they are never really satisfactory." Women are left wondering: How do we contort a whole range of feelings into these diametrical extremes? The stories we are fed don't mesh with our reality. And when we don't find ourselves reflected in the culture, we begin to doubt our observations. The consequences, though rarely articulated, are profound. "'Otherness,' in its social aspect, sets women apart from mainstream ideals and norms of behavior," Janeway warns in her seminal essay.[1]

And, when it comes to periods, women themselves may be loath to fight this attitude. Perhaps we'd rather not think about periods, let alone talk about them. After all, bleeding, by reminding women of their bodies, becomes a particularly unsavory event, since most women are not very happy with their bodies. Our bodies rarely measure up to the ideal bodies we see in magazines and on TV. And again, if our reality doesn't exist or isn't reflected in any way, it's not long before we begin to worry that there's something wrong with us, just as I began to worry that my take on menstruation was inconsequential, wrongheaded, or (worse) an affront to men.

The culture of concealment surrounding menstruation implies that there is no public place for discussing this particular "truth" about women's experience. The silence is significant on many levels. It insulates the sanitary protection industry from adequate regulation. It heightens the confusion girls experience as they struggle with the implications of their new womanhood. And, in the case of adult women, it allows the view of PMS as a scenario of emotional, hormonal-induced instability to go unchallenged. Denied a venue for discussion, the reality of menstruation remains hopelessly submerged in myth.

I have little to offer in the way of alternative scenarios. No lightbulbs have gone off in my little thought-bubble; no "Eureka!'s" have hit me, telling me plain as day what menstruation should mean to women today. Who knows what we really think or feel about periods? After all, what we know is so strongly colored by what we've been told. My sense, as I've suggested, is that women would be disinclined to celebrate their periods. But suppose menstruation were just a simple inconvenience?

I return to my modest futuristic scenario: menstruation as common cold.

"Ah-choo!"

"Bless you."

And we get on with things.

Notes

INTRODUCTION

1. Karen Houppert, "Embarrassed to Death: The Hidden Dangers of the Tampon Industry," *Village Voice*, February 7, 1995.
2. Sharon Golub, *Periods: From Menarche to Menopause* (London: Sage Publications, 1992), p. xii.

PART ONE—THE INDUSTRY

1. Barbara Ehrenreich and Deirdre English, *For Her Own Good: 150 Years of the Experts' Advice to Women* (New York: Anchor-Doubleday, 1989), p. 158.
2. Ronald H. Bailey, *Small Wonder: How Tambrands Began, Prospered, and Grew* (undated Tampax corporate history booklet published by Tambrands, Inc.), p. 14.
3. Walt Bogdanich, "House Panel Charges FDA with Neglect in Citing Danger of Dioxin in Tampons," *Wall Street Journal*, June 11, 1992, p. B8.
4. Ibid.
5. See the Environmental Protection Agency's "Health Assessment Document for 2-, 3-, 7-, 8-Tetrachlorodibenzo-p-dioxin (TCDD) and Related Compounds," August 1995. See also Joe Thornton's pamphlet *Achieving Zero Dioxin* (Greenpeace, July 1994).
6. Mary Lou Ballweg and the Endometriosis Association, *The Endometriosis Sourcebook* (Chicago: Contemporary Books, 1995), p. 370.
7. See, for example, A. Gibbons, "Dioxin Tied to Endometriosis," *Science 262* (November 26, 1993), p. 1373; M. Holloway, "An Epidemic Ignored: Endometriosis Linked to Dioxin and Immunologic Dysfunction," *Scientific American 270* (April 1994), p. 24; and Sherry E. Rier et al., "Endometriosis in Rhesus Monkeys Following Exposure to 2-, 3-, 7-, 8-Tetrachlorodibenzo-p-dioxin," *Fundamental and Applied Toxicology 21* (1993), pp. 433–441.

8. A. Mayani, S. Barel, S. Soback, and M. Almagor, *Human Reproduction* 12(2) (February 1997), pp. 373–375.

9. Ballweg, *The Endometriosis Sourcebook*, p. 389.

10. Thornton, *Achieving Zero Dioxin*, p. 15.

11. Ibid., p. 11.

12. Brigid Schulte, "Sperm Counts in U.S., Europe Declining, Report Says" (Reuters, November 24, 1997).

13. Thornton, op. cit., p. 18.

14. Carol R. Scheman, "FDA Has Confidence in Tampons' Safety" (letter to the editor), *Wall Street Journal*, July 31, 1992, p. A13.

15. EPA press release dated November 14, 1997.

16. Alecia Swasy, *Soap Opera: The Inside Story of Procter & Gamble* (New York: Simon & Schuster, 1993).

17. Philip M. Tierno, Jr., and Bruce A. Hanna, "Propensity of Tampons and Barrier Contraceptives to Amplify *Staphylococcus aureus* Toxic Shock Syndrome Toxin-1," *Infectious Diseases in Obstetrics and Gynecology 2* (July 1994), p. 140.

18. Colette Bouchez, "Little White Lies: Questions Crop Up About Tampon Safety," *New York Daily News*, May 30, 1996, p. 51.

19. *Pulp & Paper*, June 1997.

20. *Weekly Corporate Growth Report*, April 14, 1997.

21. FDA memo dated September 13, 1993.

22. Mike Boyer, "P&G Bids $2 Billion for Tampax Maker," *Cincinnati Enquirer*, April 10, 1997, p. A-1.

23. Swasy, *Soap Opera*, p. xiii.

24. "Pepper Tells Procter & Gamble Shareholders About Plans for Meeting Company Growth Goals," *PR Newswire*, October 14, 1997.

25. Jeff Harrington, "P&G Plans to Redirect Energy in Effort to Double Revenue," *Cincinnati Enquirer*, October 13, 1997, pp. 5–12, and Mike Boyer, "P&G Bids $2 Billion for Tampax Maker."

26. "P&G to Acquire Maker of Tampax Tampons for 2.88 Times Revenue," *Weekly Corporate Growth Report*, April 14, 1997.

27. Jeff Harrington, "P&G Mastering the Art of 'Globalization,'" *Cincinnati Enquirer*, April 13, 1997, p. I-1.

28. Mike Boyer, "P&G Bids $2 Billion for Tampax Maker."

29. "P&G Gambles on Tambrands," *Marketing Week*, April 17, 1997, pp. 32–33.

PART TWO—THE ADOLESCENT

1. Vern L. Bullough, "Menarche and Teenage Pregnancy: A Misuse of Historical Data," in *Menarche: The Transition from Girl to Woman*, ed. Sharon Golub (Lexington, Mass.: Lexington Books, 1983), p. 187.

2. See *Sexuality and American Social Policy: Why Have Births Among Unmarried Teens Increased?* (report by the Kaiser Family Foundation, 1997), p. 6. See also Melissa Ludtke, *On Our Own: Unmarried Motherhood in America* (New York: Random House, 1997), p. 48.

3. Kaiser Family Foundation, *Sexuality and American Social Policy*, p. vii.

4. Alan Guttmacher Institute, "The Determinants of First Sex by Age 14 in a High-Risk Adolescent Population," in *Family Planning Perspectives* (New York: Author, 1996), p. 14.

5. Bullough, op. cit., pp. 187–193.

6. Grace Wyshak, and Rose E. Frisch, "Evidence for a Secular Trend in Age of Menarche," *New England Journal of Medicine 306*, April 29, 1982, pp. 1033–1035.

7. Natalie Angier, "Chemical Tied to Fat Control Could Help Trigger Puberty," *New York Times*, January 7, 1997, p. C1.

8. Daniel Goleman, "Theory Links Early Puberty to Childhood Stress," *New York Times*, July 30, 1991, p. C1.

9. B. S. Talmey, *Genesis: A Manual for the Instruction of Children in Matters Sexual* (New York: Practitioners Publishing Company, 1910), p. 29.

10. Constance Chen, *The Sex Side of Life: Mary Ware Dennett's Pioneering Battle for Birth Control and Sex Education* (New York: New Press, 1996), p. 161.

11. William J. Robinson, *Woman: Her Sex and Love Life* (n.p.: Eugenics Publishing, 1917), p. 55.

12. For example, see Preface to Talmey's *Genesis*, pp. v–vii; the text of Mary Ware Dennett's sex-education pamphlet (found in Appendix B of Chen's *Sex Side of Life*, p. 309); and Lynda Madaras (with Area Madaras), *The What's Happening to My Body? Book For Girls* (New York: New Market Press, 1983), p. xvi.

13. A. M. Mauriceau, *The Married Woman's Private Medical Companion, Embracing the Treatment of Menstruation, or Monthly Turns, During Their Stoppage, Irregularity, or Entire Suppression; Pregnancy, and How It May Be Determined: With the Treatment of Various Diseases; Discovery to Prevent Pregnancy; the Great and Important Necessity Where Malformation or Inability Exists to Give Birth; To Prevent Miscarriage or Abortion; When Proper*

and Necessary to Effect Miscarriage, When Attended with Entire Safety;
Causes and Mode of Cure of Barrenness, or Sterility (New York: n.p., 1854),
in New York Public Library Archives: *ZAN-T3340, Reel 281.

14. See Robinson, *Woman: Her Sex and Love Life*, p. 27. See also Herman H.
Rubin, *Eugenics and Sex Harmony: The Sexes, Their Relations and Problems*
(Boston: Leslie Publishing Co., 1939), p. 158.

15. Mary Wood-Allen, *Almost a Woman* (Cooperstown, New York: Arthur H.
Crist Co., 1915), pp. 5–8.

16. Talmey, *Genesis*, p. v.

17. Ibid., pp. 11–21.

18. Emil Novak, *The Woman Asks the Doctor* (Baltimore: Williams & Wilkins,
1937), p. x.

19. *Teaching Guide to Puberty and Menstrual Health* (pamphlet by Tambrands,
Inc., 1994), p. 2.

20. See *Feminine Development* (pamphlet distributed to schools by Personal
Products, 1978), p. 16.

21. *Beauty Counter*, June 1997.

22. Talmey, op. cit., p. 25.

23. Ibid., p. 26.

24. Ibid., p. 25.

25. William Byron Forbush, *The Sex-Education of Children* (New York and
London: Funk & Wagnalls, 1919), p. 118.

26. Wood-Allen, op. cit., p. 43.

27. Novak, op. cit., p. 44.

28. Talmey, op. cit., p. 124.

29. Emily Martin, *The Woman in the Body* (Boston: Beacon Press, 1987),
p. 106.

30. Ibid., p. 46.

31. Talmey, op. cit., p. 15.

32. *A Time for Answers* (pamphlet by Tambrands, Inc., 1995), p. 15.

33. Ibid., p. 16.

34. See "The Tampax Report: A Study of Attitudes Toward Menstruation" (report conducted by Research & Forecasts, Inc. [Project Director: Peter Finn]
and underwritten by Tampax, published June 1981), p. 34.

35. Ibid., p. 37.

36. *A Time for Answers*, p. 36.

37. *Teaching Guide to Puberty and Menstrual Health*, p. 16.

38. *A Time for Answers*, p. 25.

39. Ibid., p. 27.

40. *Teaching Guide to Puberty and Menstrual Health*, p. 19.

41. Mauriceau, *The Married Woman's Private Medical Companion*, p. 75.

42. Nancy Rue, *Everything You Need to Know About Getting Your Period* (New York: Rosen, 1995), p. 20.

43. Mauriceau, op. cit., p. 7.

44. *Very Personally Yours* (booklet by Kimberly-Clark, 1981), p. 14.

45. Eric W. Johnson, *Love and Sex and Growing Up* (New York: Bantam-Skylark), 1990.

46. Lenore Williams, "Beliefs and Attitudes of Young Girls Regarding Menstruation," in *Menarche: The Transition from Girl to Woman*, ed. Sharon Golub (Lexington, Mass.: Lexington Books, 1983), pp. 139–148.

47. "Why Me?" *Teen* magazine, December 1994, December 1995, and November 1994.

48. "Why Me?" *Teen* magazine, December 1995 and February 1994.

49. *Teen* magazine, October 1994.

50. *Teen* magazine, September 1994.

51. Martin, *The Woman in the Body*, p. 97.

52. "Beauty and the Beast: How Your Period Affects Your Looks." *Mademoiselle*, June 1995, pp. 158–161.

53. Simone de Beauvoir, *The Second Sex*, tr. H. M. Parshley (New York: Random House, Vintage Books, 1974), pp. 345–350.

54. Paula Vogel, *How I Learned to Drive*, in Paula Vogel, *The Mammary Plays* (New York: Theatre Communications Group, 1998), pp. 14–18.

55. Mary Cantwell, *Manhattan, When I Was Young* (New York: Houghton Mifflin, 1995).

56. Ellen Fein and Sherrie Schneider, *The Rules: Time-Tested Secrets for Capturing the Heart of Mr. Right* (New York: Warner Books, 1997).

57. "Sexual Health Coverage in Magazines," Kaiser Family Foundation supplement to *Columbia Journalism Review*, May/June 1997.

58. Ibid., p. 1.

59. Ibid., p. 10.

60. Peggy Orenstein, *School Girls: Young Women, Self-Esteem, and the Confidence Gap* (New York: Anchor-Doubleday, 1995).

61. Mary Pipher, *Reviving Ophelia: Saving the Selves of Adolescent Girls* (New York: Grosset-Putnam, 1994).

62. Daniel Goleman, in *New York Times*, January 10, 1989, p. C-1.

63. Sharon Golub, *Periods: From Menarche to Menopause* (London: Sage Publications, 1992), pp. 38–43.

64. Ibid.

65. Judy Blume, *Are You There God? It's Me, Margaret* (New York: Bantam Doubleday Dell, 1970).

66. "All-Time Bestselling Paperback Children's Books," *Publishers Weekly*, February 5, 1996, p. 29.

67. "Top 10 Children's Books," *The Fort Worth Star-Telegram*, December 26, 1997, "Arts" section, p.3.

68. Golub, *Periods*, p. 48.

69. Stephen King, *Carrie* (New York: Signet Books, 1994), p. 8.

70. Ibid., pp. 6–8.

71. George Beahm, *The Stephen King Companion* (Kansas City: Andrews & McMeel, 1995).

72. King, *Carrie*, p. 182.

73. Anne Frank, *Anne Frank: The Diary of a Young Girl, The Definitive Edition* (New York: Anchor-Doubleday, 1995); *Anne Frank: The Diary of a Young Girl* (New York: Doubleday, 1952).

74. Cynthia Ozick, "Who Owns Anne Frank?" *The New Yorker*, October 6, 1997, pp. 76–87. See also Lawrence Graver, *An Obsession with Anne Frank: Meyer Levin and the "Diary"* (University of California Press, 1995); Ralph Melnick, *The Stolen Legacy of Anne Frank: Meyer Levin, Lillian Hellman, and the Dramatization of the Diary* (New Haven: Yale University Press, 1997); R. Zoglin, "A Darker Anne Frank," *Time* magazine, December 15, 1997, p. 110; Robert Alter, "The View From the Attic," *The New Republic*, December 4, 1995, pp. 38–42; and J. Jones, "Anne Frank Remembered," *Vogue*, December 1997, p. 176.

75. *Anne Frank, Definitive Edition*, p. 60.

76. *Anne Frank*, 1952 edition, p. 116.

77. Ibid., p. 116.

78. *Anne Frank, Definitive Edition*, p. 173.

79. Ibid., p. 175.

80. Ibid., p. 223.

81. Ibid., pp. 235–236.

82. *Anne Frank*, 1952 edition, p. 134.

83. Ibid., p. 134.

84. Ibid., p. 157.

85. Ibid., p. 56.

86. Ibid., p. 75.

87. Ibid., pp. 150–151.

88. Ibid., p. 159.

89. Ibid., p. 175.

90. Ibid., p. 185.

91. *Anne Frank, Definitive Edition*, p. 275.

92. *Anne Frank*, 1952 edition, p. 198.

93. Ibid., p. 201.
94. Ibid., p. 209.
95. Ibid., p. 225.
96. Ibid., p. 230.
97. Ibid., p. 237.

PART THREE—THE ADULT: PMS, THE SCOURGE OF THE NINETIES

1. Katharina Dalton, *Once a Month: The Original Premenstrual Handbook* (Alameda, Calif.: Hunter House/Publishers Group West, 1994), p. 101. See also Kristin Storey, *Detroit News*, December 26, 1995, p. 7; and Jean Endicott, Ellen W. Freeman, Andrea M. Kielich, and Steven J. Sondheimer, "PMS: New Treatments That Really Work," *Patient Care*, April 15, 1996, pp. 88–123.
2. As cited in *Patient Care*, April 15, 1996, p. 119.
3. The cover of Dalton's *Once a Month* brags that her self-help book alone has sold over 200,000 copies; PMS Access president Marla Ahlgrimm says that PMS Access's 800-number hotline logs more than three thousand calls a month.
4. Joseph Martorano, and Maureen Morgan, with William Fryer, *Unmasking PMS: The Complete PMS Medical Treatment Plan* (New York: Evans and Co., 1993); Stephanie DeGraff Bender and Kathleen Kelleher: *PMS: Women Tell Women How to Control Premenstrual Syndrome* (originally titled *PMS: A Positive Program to Gain Control*). Oakland, California, New Harbinger Publications, 1996.
5. See PMS Access's booklet *The Odds Are Almost Even*, p. 4.
6. Sharon Lerner, "Are the Treatment Options for PMS Leaving You Bloated, Irritable, and Crampy?" *Ms.* magazine, July/August 1996, pp. 38–41.
7. Dalton, *Once a Month*, p. 115.
8. Ibid., p. 3.
9. Ibid., pp. 115–116.
10. Ibid., p. 120.
11. Ibid., pp. 124–125.
12. Ibid., p. 107.
13. Ibid., p. 108.
14. Ibid., p. 111.
15. Ibid., p. 117.
16. Cited in Leta Stetter Hollingworth, *Functional Periodicity: An Experimental Study of the Mental and Motor Abilities of Women During Menstruation* (New York: Teachers College Columbia University Press, 1914), p. 29.

17. Barbara Ehrenreich and Deirdre English, *For Her Own Good: 150 Years of the Experts' Advice to Women* (New York: Anchor-Doubleday, 1989), pp. 123–124.

18. Hollingworth, *Functional Periodicity*, p. 97.

19. Ibid., p. 95.

20. Helen Rogan, *Mixed Company: Women in the Modern Army* (New York: Putnam, 1981), p.135.

21. See Ehrenreich, *For Her Own Good*, p. 125; *Psychiatric Annals* 26(9), September 1996, p. 573; *Patient Care*, April 15, 1996, p. 95; and Dalton, *Once a Month*.

22. Dalton, *Once a Month*, p. 212.

23. *Psychiatric Annals* 26(9), September 1996, p. 578.

24. W. Freeman, K. Rickels, S. J. Sondheimer, and M. Polansky, "A Double-Blind Trial of Oral Progesterone, Alprazolam, and Placebo in Treatment of Severe Premenstrual Syndrome," *Journal of the American Medical Association* 274(1), 1995, p. 51.

25. Boston Women's Health Book Collective, *Our Bodies, Our Selves: A Book by and for Women* (New York: Touchstone-Simon & Schuster, 1992), p. 252.

26. Bender and Kelleher, *PMS*, p. 111.

27. Dalton, *Once a Month*, pp. 104–105.

28. Catherine Bennett, "In the Blood or In the Head?" *The Guardian*, June 1, 1993, p. 2.

29. Bender and Kelleher, *PMS*, p. 52.

30. Ibid., p. 65.

31. Ibid., p. 94.

32. Ibid., p. 150.

33. Golub, *Periods*, p. 204.

34. Ibid., p. 75.

35. J. M. Siegel, J. H. Johnson, and I. G. Sarason, "Life Changes and Menstrual Discomfort," *Journal of Human Stress* 5 (1979), pp. 41–46.

36. Sharon Golub, "The Effect of Premenstrual Anxiety and Depression on Cognitive Function," *Journal of Personality and Social Psychology* 34 (1976), pp. 99–104; "The Magnitude of Premenstrual Anxiety and Depression," *Psychosomatic Medicine* 34 (1976), pp. 4–14.

37. A. S. Rossi and P. E. Rossi, "Body Time and Social Time: Mood Patterns by Menstrual Cycle Time and Day of Week," *Social Science Research* 6 (1977), pp. 273–308.

38. Karen Paige, "Women Learn to Sing the Menstrual Blues," *Psychology Today*, September 1973, p. 49.

39. Golub, *Periods*, p. 204.
40. Meir Steiner, "Fluoxetine in the Treatment of Premenstrual Dysphoria," *New England Journal of Medicine* 332 (June 1995), pp. 1529–1534.
41. See *Psychiatric Annals* 26(9) (September 1996), p. 569.
42. "That Time of Month," *The Economist*, July 31, 1993, p. 75.
43. Heather Nash and Joan Chrisler, "The Effect of the Presence of Premenstrual Dysphoric Disorder in the DSM-IV on the Perception of Premenstrual Changes," in *Proceedings of the Eleventh Biannual Conference of the Society for Menstrual Cycle Research*, June 1995, Montreal, Canada, pp. 266–308.
44. Peter Kramer, *Listening to Prozac* (New York: Penguin, 1993), p. 15.
45. Ibid., p. 23.
46. Ibid., p. 31.
47. Ibid., p. 27.
48. Ibid., p. 254.

PART FOUR—UNLIKELY PROPHETS:
THE MENSTRUAL COUNTERCULTURE

1. Karen and Jennifer Gravelle, *The Period Book: Everything You Don't Want to Ask (But Need To Know)* (New York: Walker Publishing Company, 1996), p. 85.
2. Ibid., p. 93.
3. Ibid., pp. 52–93.
4. Ibid., pp. 70–71.
5. Ibid., p. 71.
6. Kathleen O'Grady and Paula Wansbrough, *Sweet Secrets: Stories of Menstruation* (Toronto: Second Story Press, 1997), p. 80.
7. Ibid., p. 137.
8. Lynda Madaras (with Area Madaras), *The What's Happening to My Body? Book For Girls* (New York: Newmarket Press, 1988), p. xvii.
9. Ibid., p. 104.
10. Ibid., p. 129.
11. Ibid., p. 249.
12. L. L. Rogers, G. A. Wilker, and S. S. Scott, "Reactions of Black Bears to Human Menstrual Odors," *Journal of Wildlife Management* 55(4), 1991, pp. 632–634.
13. See Anastasia Toufexis, "A Woman's Best Defense? A Maverick Scientist Contends That Menstruation Protects Against Infection," *Time* magazine, October 4, 1993, pp. 72–73.

14. Jennifer Stonier, "Bloodless Time," in *Proceedings of the Eleventh Biannual Conference of the Society for Menstrual Cycle Research*, pp. 71–79.

15. Penelope Shuttle and Peter Redgrove, *The Wise Wound: The Myths, Realities, and Meanings of Menstruation* (New York: Grove Press, 1978), p. 285.

16. Ibid., p. 282.

17. Ibid., p. 15.

CONCLUSION

1. Elizabeth Janeway, "Who Is Sylvia?: On the Loss of Sexual Paradigms," *Signs: Journal of Women in Culture and Society 5*, Summer 1980. See also *Women: Sex and Sexuality*, ed. Catharine R. Stimpson and Ethel Spector Person (Chicago and London: University of Chicago Press, 1980), pp. 4–20.

Acknowledgments

I would like to thank the following people for their help with this book: Elisabeth Kallick Dyssegaard, for her confidence in this project and for gently shepherding me from indignation to analysis; Amy Virshup, for her predictably insightful and thorough comentary on sections of this book; Cindi Leive, for tipping me off about the "period stories" in teen magazines and for her meticulous reading of various chapters; Eva Lewandowski, for letting me interview her campers; Lisa Kennedy and Karen Durbin, for enthusiastically editing my first investigation into the sanitary protection industry; my feminist reading group—Lucia Russett, Sandy Opatow, Katherine Pushkar, Cindi Leive, and Karen Cook—for exploring so many of these ideas with me; Sue Breton, for her intellectual and concrete contributions; Sandra Dijkstra, my agent, for never batting an eye at this "peculiar" book proposal and for peddling it with similar aplomb; Sharon Golub, for suggesting sources and for her inspirational years of work researching this neglected topic; Joe Cummins and Jenny Douglas, for their incisive editorial suggestions; Pat Houppert, for her intellectual support (reading and commenting on various drafts), her financial support (the occasional "artist's grants"), and her practical support (serving as baby-sitting pinch hitter extraordinaire); Abby Kagan and Elaine Blair, for their valued contributions to the final product; Darla Batistic, for tossing around some of these thoughts with me for the past twenty years; and Stephen Nunns, my reluctant yet trenchant and indispensable critic.

Permissions

Grateful acknowledgment is made for permission to reprint the following:

Illustrations
"Welcome This New Day for Womanhood," 1936 Tampax ad by Procter & Gamble

1934 fall/winter Sears catalog, page 258, by Sears, Roebuck and Co.

"How Could You Do This to Me, Mom?!" 1998 Always ad by Procter & Gamble

"PMS Escape" 1998 package by IntraNutria

"Your Body Understood It on the Day You Were Born," 1988 inSync ad by A-Fem Medical Corporation

"Between Us," 1996 Carefree ad by Personal Products Corporation

Excerpts
From *The Second Sex* by Simone de Beauvoir. Copyright © 1974 by Simone de Beauvoir, translated by H. M. Parshley. Used by permission of Alfred A. Knopf.

Index